THE MUST-HAVE WEIGHT LOSS GUIDE

*The Proven Ways to Burn Stubborn Body Fats,
Detox, and Reset the Body*

BARBARA SMITH

THE MUST-HAVE
WEIGHT LOSS GUIDE

TABLE OF CONTENTS

INTRODUCTION

Almost everyone has their own story, or at the very least, a view on weight loss. It is also a fact that almost everyone has a significant interest in weight loss. Sadly, a good majority of the population still struggle with their weight and need assistance.

According to studies, there are about 11,100,000 google searches on the words "weight loss" monthly. Yes, you read that right. That is just monthly statistics. This means that an unbelievable average of 120 million searches is expected at the end of the year. This fact only affirms the great importance of the topic and why this '***Must-Have Weight Loss Guide***' is indeed a must-have and is very much needed.

This Must-Have Weight Loss Guide is very well detailed and contains all there is to know about weight loss. It comprises seven chapters divided into two parts; the first part containing the first three chapters introduces you to the guide, helps you understand your body better, and finally introduces you to weight loss, starting with weight gain. The second part of this guide comprising the last four chapters will focus on the proven ways to burn body fats and detox, and reset the body. Three approaches to effectively losing weight – dietary prescription, lifestyle intervention, and exercise solutions, will be critically discussed.

Finally, you will be taught how to create the best routine to help you shed those extra pounds. Sit back and get ready to be brought into this world of knowledge expertly designed with so much professionalism.

PURPOSE OF GUIDE

Weight loss has become an international topic, and everyone has their own opinion. It could be that even yourself have had various personal struggles in trying to attain your ideal weight, or maybe you are a worker in a company that offers help to people looking to lose weight. It could even be that you are a personal trainer or coach, a healthcare professional, or someone just looking to gain general knowledge on the topic to have a few tips under your belt. You may also be preparing for a workshop on weight loss and need some points to present. Whatever category you belong to, you must have a little knowledge of this topic or at least have your own opinion. However, it is best for you if you go for a professional's opinion. This is why I, with all my expert knowledge and training, alongside my unique perspective and personal story and observations, have taken out time to work on this project to help you lose those extra pounds.

Weight loss success stories are quite much out there, but this Must Have Weight Loss Guide offers many more than just motivational stories. You get to learn and understand your body, how weight is gained, and finally, how to lose it using the best tested and trusted methods there are. These methods are expertly reviewed step-by-step procedure that is relatively very easy to understand and follow.

You are also given all you need to draft and start a weight loss program all on your own. It is indeed a complete package. Get ready to lose some weight!

What to Expect from Using This Guide

Before you start this guide, I would like you to have a clear understanding of what you will benefit from this guide. Below is a detailed explanation of everything you stand to gain or simply what you should expect from making use of this guide:

- According to results and statistics from multiple studies, effectively losing weight doesn't just reduce your risk factor but also your entire risk factor profile. You gain steady improvement health-wise, as weight loss moves from modest to substantial on a scale.

- As you follow this guide, your eyesight will also improve. This is confirmed from testimonies and personal experience. People who have followed my guides in the past have testified of having improved vision.

- You will gain the ability to sleep well as you follow the diet plans and other techniques listed here. You will also overcome problems relating to sleep apnea.

- There will be a significant boost in your immune system.

- Your blood will begin to experience purification.
- Most obviously, you will lose extra fat. The fats in the waist, stomach, thighs, and butts are perfect examples of the most probable parts you'll lose fat.
- Every problem relating to fatty lumps around the body will be settled, and all these lumps will be dissolved by following my tips.
- Following this guide will not only boost your sex life and stamina but will improve your looks and sex appeal as well.
- Losing weight on its own automatically boosts blood circulation. This is basically because cholesterol is reduced from your blood vessels. Also, the penis size will see a notable increase as the blood vessels become healthier, and your heart can effectively pump blood to those parts.
- Your skin begins to glow, and since extra fatty cells in the face are lost, you will have an uplifted facial look.
- Research shows that 90% of diabetes, 80% of heart diseases, and 60% of cancer can be prevented from losing weight. Following these steps helps increase these chances even further.
- My guide will help to keep your blood pressure at a normal level, eliminating the need for blood pressure-related drugs.
- All coronary heart diseases can also be prevented.

- You will be free from stomach-related gastroesophageal reflux disease.
- All problems related to osteoarthritis will be taken care of.
- As extra cholesterol will be removed from your body, you will live a risk-free life from heart attacks. This is mainly because your veins will be cleansed and become healthy.
- You will be saved from many skin-related diseases as well.
- You can enjoy this world more, as you get to live a healthier life, and about 8-10 years is added to your life.
- Obesity has become a major cause of headache for many people in our modern world today. Due to its expensive treatment, obese people are subjected to excessive spending as weight loss treatment can cost quite a lot. However, my guide will provide you with more than you will get from regular treatments and for far less cost.
- All-round good health.

Understanding Your Body

The human body is quite complex, but it can be described simply as a highly organized structure composed of many unique units that complement each other and perform specific functions necessary for the sustenance of life. In the simplest term, the human body is just everything that you are made up of.

It would be best if you understand your body's physiology (or how your body functions) and its anatomy (how it is structured) so that you can digest everything on this guide as smoothly as possible.

Have it in mind that this is not an anatomy and physiology course. It is rather just a walkthrough of terms that I believe you should be familiar with before starting the main business. With that said, let's begin!

A Brief Anatomy of The Human Body

The most fundamental parts of the body, as well all know, are the head, neck, torso, arms, and legs. To save you time, instead of going through all the parts of the human body, we will discuss the systems instead. This is so you fully understand what goes on in your body, and hence why losing some weight shouldn't be underrated.

The human body comprises various biological systems that carry out some specific functions that are essential for our everyday living.

Circulatory System: Its main job is transportation. It is made up of body parts like the heart, blood, blood vessels, arteries, and veins. It is responsible for the transport of blood, oxygen, carbon dioxide, nutrients, and hormones.

Digestive System: The digestive system is composed of a connected series of organs such as the mouth, esophagus, stomach, small and large intestines, rectum down to the anus. They all work together to facilitate the breakdown and absorption of food and remove waste afterward. The liver and pancreas also contribute significantly by producing digestive juices.

Endocrine System: This system is responsible for the secretion of hormones. It is composed of all the eight major glands that are responsible for secreting hormones. When these hormones are secreted, they travel to different tissues and carry out specific functions that are needed in the body. These functions include metabolism, growth, and sexual function.

Immune System: This can be referred to as the line of defense of the body. It is responsible for protecting the body from bacteria, viruses and other pathogens that may be harmful, hence, acting as a defense against infections, sicknesses, and diseases. The immune system is made up of lymph nodes, bone marrow, the spleen, lymphocytes (including B and T-cells), the thymus, and leukocytes (white blood cells)

Lymphatic System: It is responsible for making and moving lymph. Lymph is a clear fluid that contains white blood cells. Hence, the lymphatic system also plays a role in defense of the body. Another vital role this system plays is removing excess lymph fluid from bodily tissues, returning it to the blood.

Nervous System: This is the system responsible for controlling voluntary actions and involuntary actions and sending signals to various parts of the body. It is further separated into the central nervous system and the peripheral nervous system. The former consists of the brain and spinal cord, while the latter comprises nerves that connect to every other part of the body.

Muscular System: This system comprises about 650 muscles that aid in movement, blood flow, and other bodily functions. Muscles are divided into three parts viz. skeletal muscle (connected to the bone and assists involuntary movements), smooth muscles (found in organs and aids the movement of substances through them), and cardiac muscles (found in the heart and facilitates the pumping of blood).

Reproductive System: The reproductive system contains all that is necessary for reproduction. This includes the male reproductive system (penis and testes producing sperm) and the female reproductive system (vagina, uterus and ovaries, producing eggs). They both work hand-in-hand to produce a fertilized egg that grows into the fetus, producing life.

Skeletal System: This is the system that aids our movements and blood cells production and calcium storage. It consists of 206 bones that are all connected by tendons, ligaments, and cartilages. The teeth are also part of this system.

Respiratory System: This is vital for the intake of oxygen and the expulsion of carbon dioxide, thereby facilitating breathing. It consists of the organs and body parts that aids breathing and respiration in general. Examples of these are the trachea, diaphragm and lungs.

Urinary System: This system helps in the expulsion of urea (a waste product from the body's breakdown of certain foods). It is made up of both kidneys, both ureters, the bladder, two sphincter muscles and the urethra. Urine is produced by the kidneys and goes to the bladder via the ureters and expels through the urethra.

Skin or Integumentary System: This system is made up of the largest organ, the skin and its various components, and the hair and nails. It is responsible for the protection of the internal organs from external physical threats. It is the first line of defense against viruses, bacteria and other pathogens. The skin also carries out other functions such as temperature regulation and waste elimination through perspiration. The human body consists of five vital organs, which are essential for survival. These organs include the brain, heart, liver, kidneys, and lungs.

The brain is referred to as the control center of the body and is responsible for sending and receiving signals to other organs through the nervous system and secreted hormones. It also helps in thinking, feelings, memory, intelligence and the perception of the world. The heart's only and vital function is to pump blood and facilitate its circulation throughout the body. The lungs, which slightly envelop the heart, function to absorb oxygen from the environment into the body for use and remove carbon dioxide from the body to the environment.

The liver is also vital and carries out many essential functions. These functions include detoxification of harmful chemicals, breakdown of drugs, filtration of blood, bile secretion, and blood clotting proteins' production.

The kidneys are equally important and assists in the removal of waste and extra fluid from the blood. The kidney excretes urea by combining it with other substances to make urine and expel everything through the urethra.

Why We Should Keep Our Body in Good Shape and Good Condition

As we have seen earlier, our bodies' internal part plays a crucial role in our lives. Equally, the exterior parts are also very important as both complement each other perfectly. Hence, it is in our best interest to keep our bodies healthy.

It is rather well-known that living an active lifestyle plays a major role in making you have a better outlook and feelings, despite your activity level. When it comes to why we should keep our body in shape, there could be more to it than the reason for a better look/feeling. It could just be to stay healthy, make significant improvements, get ready for an event, or even just for fun. However, these are just personal opinions. There are some certain general reasons for or benefits to keeping your fit and healthy.

It Reduces Your Dementia Risk: In recent times, it has been found out that staying active can decrease the risk of dementia as your mind function and energy are boosted. Carrying out physical activities more often helps increase cognitive function, especially in healthy elderly persons, thereby potentially reducing the risk of getting cognitive impairment. Activities which you will need learning skills like memory and concentration (for example, dance classes) are beneficial for people who have an increased risk of Alzheimer's disease.

It Decreases Your Osteoporosis Risk: Keeping your body fit, most especially through the use of weight-bearing exercises, is very beneficial for bone health. From my years of experience as a personal trainer, I have seen that exercises are, in fact, one of the best ways of preventing osteoporosis and maintaining your bone mass. Some exercises that we will be discussing in the later stages of this guide are the best for this.

It Aids in the Improvement of Your Sex Life: Performing exercises regularly helps in increasing your libido. In fact, when your carryout exercises, your brain produces endorphins which facilitate the release of sex hormones. Aside from boosting your sexual performance, these hormones reduce your heart rate and blood pressure and cortisol levels, improve digestion, and help in the body's relaxation.

For the Prevention of Muscle Loss: Earlier, we discussed just how important the muscular systems are. However, as well as grow older, there is less efficiency in building muscle by the body. Also, the muscles that have already been built breaks down faster. Due to this, keeping fit is so much more important for healthy aging. Regular exercises will help in the increase and maintenance of muscle mass. As your metabolism is kept high, you are given strength and endurance to help in your everyday life.

For Improved Digestion: When your body is kept fit, intestinal muscles' activities break down food and carry out the movement of the broken-down food to their respective parts and systems. With strengthened abdominal muscles, sluggishness is minimized.

Reduction of Stress, Depression and Anxiety: You must have been told that regular exercises boost your mood. When you carry out regular exercises, neurotransmitters and endorphins are released, and this helps eases depression. Also, your body temperature is raised, which calms down your nerves. Another point worth mentioning is that if you are to achieve your perfect body goals, you will gain more self-confidence, which is very important in reducing stress, depression and anxiety.

Risk of Cancer is Significantly Reduced: According to various studies, regular exercises have been seen to greatly reduce cancers of the lungs, colon and breast as active people are at lower risk of them. A study conducted in 2007 even shows that a high level of estrogen (stored in fat) increases the risk of breast cancer, and therefore, regular exercises is a crucial step forward for its prevention.

Improvement of Your Skin: From experience, I have seen that glowing skin is a top motivator for many people wishing to get in shape, common most especially with the ladies. Well, whoever you are, if you are looking for a better skin tone, then you should definitely start working towards regular exercises. For a fact, exercise helps in enhancing the flow of blood to and throughout your skin. Also, regular exercises control the excessive secretion of acne-inducing testosterone hormones such as DHEA and DHT, thereby improving acne. Besides, sweating unclogs pores, clearing up space for breakouts, resulting in the detoxification of oil and dirt from the skin.

Enhancement of Mental Performance and Work Productivity: Employing my professionalism, I can boldly tell you that exercise is vital for improving the overall quality of life, especially when working. Besides the fact that your self-confidence is boosted, even in your workplace, helping you take on leadership roles and improving performance, your overall productivity and focus are significantly enhanced.

Finding a New Circle of Friends: If you are to take your fitness activities to the level of joining a fitness club, you not only receive help and guidance from professionals, but you get to meet people with common goals with you. This will help boost your social life and give you all the motivation you need to complete your fitness journey.

Also, as your confidence is boosted, you achieve your goals even much faster.

WEIGHT GAIN

As a seasoned professional, I believe that you need to understand the problem before proffering the solution. This is why I will take you through everything you are expected to know about weight gain before starting weight loss practices.

Weight, in physical science, is explained as the force exerted on a body by gravity. Its formula is $W = mg$ (where W = weight, m = mass of object, and g = acceleration due to gravity). However, the weight we will be discussing here is related to the mass of human bodies.

Body Mass Index (BMI) is simply the weight of a person in kilograms over the square of the person's height in meters. The BMI is a cheap and easy method for screening weight category. These categories are underweight, healthy weight, overweight and obese. BMI does not directly measure a person's fat, but it is averagely correlated with more direct body fat measures. Also, BMI can be as accurate in measuring various metabolic disease outcomes as the other direct measures. There are other methods to measure body fatness, but they are not always available as they require professionals or are too expensive.

Weight gain is basically just an increase in the bodyweight of an individual. It usually entails increased muscle mass, fat deposits, excess fluids like water, and many other factors. Gaining body weight is a rather slow process, as it does not take days and weeks but months and years instead. Weight is gained when the calories you get from the food you consume exceed the number of calories you burn for energy in carrying out your daily activities. This leads to an excess of unwanted calories, which are then converted and stored as fats. When this process continues to occur for a long time, you will accumulate many more calories and hence weight over time.

Weight gain has become a huge problem, and In the United States, the prevalence of adult obese status (adults with BMI greater than or equal to 30 kg/m^2) has seen a massive rise since the 1970s. Recently, the rate of obesity has been rising even in women above the age of 60. This clearly calls for attention, and in this chapter, I will help you understand all there are to weight gain.

Main Factors That Causes Weight Gain

We have seen weight gain, especially obesity, to be one of the world's biggest health problems today. This problem is most often related to several conditions such as elevated blood sugar, a poor lipid profile and high blood pressure. These conditions are altogether known as metabolic syndrome. Compared to people with weight in the normal range, those with this metabolic syndrome stand a much higher chance of suffering from heart disease and type 2 diabetes.

Due to the occurrences of this syndrome, many kinds of research have been dedicated to finding the causes of obesity or weight gain in general and how one can prevent it or cure it if they are already experiencing it.

Many people believe that weight gain and obesity are caused solely by a lack of willpower. This is, however, not entirely correct because a lot more factors than that could cause weight gain. I can agree that in most cases, the problem is caused by eating behavior and lifestyle as some people find it very difficult to control their eating habits. However, overeating can result from various biological factors like genetics and hormones, and others are just predisposed to gain weight.

I am not saying that people cannot overcome their genetic disadvantages because I'd be wrong. People sure can simply by changing their lifestyle and behavior through willpower, dedication and perseverance. But saying that behavior is purely a function of willpower is far too simplistic. This claim doesn't consider all the other factors, and these factors are critical in determining what people do and when they do it. Below are 10 major factors that cause weight gain, obesity and metabolic syndrome diseases:

Genetics: This is a compelling determining factor of obesity. Children of parents who are obese or who have much weight are more prone to becoming obese than children of lean parents. This does not entirely mean that obesity is totally predetermined. What we take in and how we eat in general definitely has a major effect on which genes are expressed and which are not. There are certain classes of food in certain balances which you can eat despite your genes, and you will deal with weight gain, preventing or curing it even if you have obese parents.

Another way in which obese genes can be expressed is in non-industrialization. Societies experiencing this tend to become obese fast as they are usually known to consume a typical western diet. If these diets are to affect their genes, they stand a higher chance of suffering from obesity. This doesn't mean that their genes changed; it's just that their environment played a major role in determining the signals that are sent to the genes.

Engineered Junk Foods: Foods that go through heavy processes are usually a mixture of refined ingredients and additives. This makes the products' selling point, their meager prices, long-lasting nature, and their great taste even after staying so long. As these foods are being made as tasty as possible, sales are increased, which means more money for the manufacturers. However, they are also promoting over-eating and potentially a rise in the cases of obesity. Most processed foods are not even anything close to whole foods. They are not manufactured and sold to provide nutrients, but rather, they are engineered with the sole purpose of getting people addicted, ignoring their general well-being. Although they are safe in the sense that they are not poisonous, they are not good for our health. Unfortunately, stores today are filled with these processed foods, promoting overeating, thereby causing weight gain.

Food Addiction: Weight gain is usually caused as the reward centers in your brain are often stimulated by many sugar-sweetened, high-fat junk foods, thereby causing a severe addiction. In fact, several people compare these foods to drugs that are frequently abused, such as; alcohol, nicotine, cocaine, and cannabis.

Junk foods especially cause addiction in vulnerable people. When this happens, the victims lose control over their eating behavior and start overeating unnecessarily. This occurrence is similar to people who lose control over their drinking behavior as they struggle with alcohol addiction.

Addiction, in particular, is a serious issue and can be really hard to overcome. When you're addicted, it is the brain itself that is affected, and you lose your conscious freedom of choice. Fortunately, the difficulty isn't impossibility, as it is possible to break free from addiction. Stick to this guide for more help on your addiction.

Aggressive Marketing: Some companies make misleading claims just to make huge profits. They sell out products that are harmful to health and make it seem like a good thing. An example of this is Junk food producers.

It should not seem like I'm over criticizing junk foods. But the thing is, junk foods are, in fact, a major cause of weight gain. Also, many producers of junk foods and other related products sometimes use unethical tactics just to market these goods.

The worst part is that their main target is children. And this is very bad because in our world today, the cases of obesity, diabetes and addiction to junk foods are high, long before these kids who lack the knowledge and experience become old enough to make an informed decision. This plays a crucial role in weight gain.

Insulin: This is an essential hormone that helps mainly in regulating energy storage. One of its functions is informing fat cells when to store fat or holding on to the one they already have. Many western diets contain ingredients that promote insulin resistance. And this can be especially disadvantageous for overweight and obese individuals.

When certain products promote insulin levels in the body, more energy, which should have been available for use, gets stored in fat cells, thereby leading to weight gain.

One of the best ways this problem can be checked is to reduce refined carbohydrates intake and focus more on fiber intake. This way, you experience an automatic reduction in calorie intake, hence losing weight without any effort.

Certain Medications: There are several pharmaceutical drugs we use, which have weight gain as a side effect. A good example is antidepressants which have been blamed for many causes of weight gain over time. Other famous examples are diabetes medication, and antipsychotics. These drugs do not affect you mentally, like reducing your willpower. Rather, they work by altering your body and brain's functioning as they decrease metabolic rate or increase appetite.

Leptin Resistance: This is another hormone that contributes a lot to weight gain. Fat cells are responsible for Leptin's production, and the blood levels in them increase as there is a higher fat mass. Due to this, the level of Leptin in obese people is very high. In healthy people, on the other hand, the only time Leptin is high is when they are suffering from reduced appetite. However, when they are working properly, they play a major role by telling your brain how high your fat store is.

The main issue obese people have with leptin is that this important hormone doesn't work best in their bodies because it finds it difficult to cross their blood-brain barrier. This condition is commonly referred to as leptin resistance and is one of the main factors in the pathogenesis of obesity. This is because the appetite-reducing hormones don't function well in obese patients, ultimately making them gain more weight.

Food Availability: This is one factor in particular which dramatically influences people's tendency to gain weight. Fortunately, but yet, unfortunately, food availability in the U.S., in particular, have become very high over the years. Although this has more pros than cons, however, it has greatly influenced overfeeding. Another issue that makes this even worse is that this occurrence has brought about a massive increase in the circulation of unhealthy products such as junk foods. Many convenience stores now choose to market food items, making them more money, ignoring the health benefits or hazards the products might pose.

This problem is even more expressed in a poorer neighborhood where unhealthy foods are cheaper than healthy whole foods, and where people don't even have options of purchasing real foods and fresh vegetables as most of the stores in these regions have opted to go for sodas, candy, and processed packaged junk foods.

Added Sugar: Added sugar may just be the single worst aspect of the modern diet. I say this because excess sugar consumption is responsible for various changes in the hormones and biochemistry of your body. This ultimately contributes to weight gain as well.

Added sugar is basically just half glucose, half fructose. Glucose is gotten from many foods such as starches, while fructose is gotten majorly from added sugar. Excess intake of fructose is bad for our health as it causes insulin resistance and heightened insulin levels. Also, how it promotes satiety is nowhere close to the way glucose does. It is for these reasons that excessive sugar intake is one of the main factors of obesity.

Misinformation: Information has become a mighty instrument in our world today. It is vital in determining how many things turn out. The type of information you get influences your decisions and hence your entire life. This just means that getting the wrong information can be disastrous to you in many ways. Unfortunately, people all over the world today are often being misinformed about issues relating to their health and nutrition.

There are many reasons for this, but the problem depends mainly on where this information is gotten. Many websites on the Internet now spread incorrect information on health and nutrition issues, while some news outlets tend to oversimplify or misinterpret the research results.

Some misinformation can be blamed on old and outdated theories. Another major role player is good companies who are looking to market their products.

Finally, if your weight-loss strategies are based on false information, it may become challenging for you to progress. With that said, we have seen that misinformation can contribute a great deal to weight gain, and at the same time, make weight loss even more difficult. The major reason why you should carefully choose your sources.

Everything stated above is affirming that there are a wide variety of factors that play major roles in weight gain, many of which have nothing to do with willpower. Therefore, you should not feel hopeless about your condition because willpower may not be the main cause of weight gain; it is definitely essential in losing weight.

HEALTH RISKS OF WEIGHT GAIN

The disadvantages associated with weight gain are too many to mention. Therefore, we will stick only to the health hazards and risks which gaining too much weight poses.

Type 2 Diabetes: This is a disease where blood sugar levels are above normal, which is a major cause of many other diseases, making it very deadly. Studies in 2009 showed that diabetes was ranked seventh as the leading cause of death in the U.S. Also, above 87% of victims of cases of diabetes were overweight or obese people.

High Blood Pressure: Blood pressure is how hard your blood is pumped through arteries and how it pushes against their walls when moving to the rest of your body each time your heartbeats. Although High Blood Pressure (or hypertension) often has no symptoms, it could lead to deadly issues like stroke, heart disease, and kidney failure. High blood pressure is related to obesity as the heart of an obese individual needs to pump harder to reach all their cells.

Heart Disease: This is a general term used for describing problems that affect your heart. Its main cause is when a blood vessel carrying blood to the heart becomes hard and narrow. This may result in the heart not getting enough blood. Heart diseases, in turn, may lead to angina (chest pain), heart attack, heart failure, or sudden cardiac death. The disease of the heart is one of the leading causes of death in the U.S.

Overweight or obese people usually have other health problems such as high blood pressure, high blood sugar, and high cholesterol, increasing heart disease risk.

Cancer: This is when cells in onepart of the body grow abnormally or out of control. The cancerous cells often spread to other body parts. In the U.S., cancer is one of the leading causes of death. Adding body fats to yourself increases the risk of several cancers.

Sleep Apnea: This is a condition where victims suffer one or more breathing pauses during sleep. This can, in turn, lead to sleepiness during the day, difficulty in focusing, and even heart failure. Obesity increases the risk of sleep apnea the most. When fats are stored around the neck, it may make the airway smaller.

Osteoarthritis: It is a common health problem that causes stiffness, and hence pain in the joints. Having extra weight may place extra pressure on joints and cartilages.

Kidney Disease: The kidney is responsible for blood filtration, extra water removal, and removal of waste products such as urea. It also helps control blood pressure. Kidney disease damages the kidney, making it less effective in carrying out its activities. Obesity causes an increase in the risk of diabetes and high blood pressure, which are the most common causes of chronic kidney disease.

Pregnancy Problems: Obese and overweight women are at great risk of developing gestational diabetes or high blood sugar during pregnancy. They are also at great risk of having pre-eclampsia or high blood pressure during pregnancy which is a problem for both mother and baby if not treated.

Another pregnancy problem of being overweight or obese is the heightened risk of being born too soon, being stillborn, and having neural tube effects.

Overweight pregnant women are prone to have high blood sugar, high blood pressure, or to develop insulin resistance. They also increase the risks of surgery and anesthesia. Severe obesity increases the time taken for surgery and results in blood loss.

These are all just a few problems associated with gaining too much weight. There are other mental, physical and societal problems that you can always research on your own. For now, we have to move forward.

Carbohydrates and Fats

Aside from the many factors that cause weight gain, two classes of food, in particular, are generally blamed for being the major cause of weight gain. These are Carbohydrates and Fats, and we will learn everything relevant to it.

Carbohydrates, also known as carbs, are rather very confusing. Some sources claim that eating carbohydrates causes weight gain, while others debunk this; saying it is an essential part of our diets.

However, I am telling you that despite those two conflicting pieces of advice, carbohydrates are, in fact, not responding to weight gain by themselves. That is caused by excess calories and not generalizing as the entire carbohydrates. Therefore, when it comes to carbohydrates and weight gain, all that matters, or the only factors that involve weight gain are the type and amount of carbs consumed and whatever you use as an alternative to them. Further on, I will tell you more about carbohydrates, so you know how to enjoy them without fear of gaining weight.

Carbohydrates are an essential class of food that is converted by the body to glucose / stored as glycogen, itsupply energy to our bodies for our daily activities. Carbohydrates are, in fact, the main source of energy for the body.

The U.S. Department of Health & Human Services recommended that the adults' total intake of calories should have 45 – 65% coming from carbs, while the remaining comes from protein and fats. These three (carbohydrates, proteins and fats) are collectively known as the macronutrients, which are essential for your body's optimal functioning.

Carbohydrates are of different types; Complex carbs can be found naturally in whole foods. Refined carbs, on the other hand, are manufactured along with processed food. Even though it is not entirely correct to differentiate between "good" or "bad" food, it is wise to have it in mind that all carbs are created differently and are therefore not equal. This means that some exist in formsthat are more beneficial to you and your health than others.

Complex Carbs: Complex carbs usually have high fiber content. It requires a relatively long time for them to be digested than other carbs. This also means that they give you a feeling of satisfaction and keep you full longer. Hence, you won't be having the physical need for food within that time. The total amount of carbs you eat should be mostly complex. The following are few examples of foods that contain complex carbs; Beans, Oats, Potatoes, Green Veggies, Whole grains, etc. This also means that whole-wheat bread has many more complex carbs than white ones, and white rice has less than brown rice.

Refined Carbs: These are found in excess in processed foods like white bread and cakes. During the processing of these foods, a huge portion of their natural fiber and other nutrients are lost, leaving them with a good amount of sugary carbs and empty calories, which is the major source of weight gain. To make it even worse, the processing of refined carbs by your body is very fast, meaning you'll get hungry quickly; therefore, you will be eating more throughout the day. Examples of foods that contain refined carbs are; Bread, Pastries, and Pasta.

Moving further, the one thing that will be on your mind now is **how carbs impact weight**. Well, the fact is that they don't cause an instant weight gain. However, carbs which are of high starch content are usually dense with calories. Therefore, you should definitely be mindful of your intake to avoid unnecessary weight gain.

When consuming carbs, another thing you need to understand is the basic processes required. First, you need to find a healthy balance for yourself. In fact, finding the right balance is one of the most important parts of eating carbs. We know it's not right if your meal contains only carbs; however, it's also as much of a problem if you're leaving them out of your meals completely.

For some time, diets which have a low content of carbohydrates have been popular for weight loss. Aside from that, these methods have their drawbacks; there is no guarantee that any of them will make you lose weight. We experts sometimes question the safety of diets with very low carbohydrate content as they have a notable risk of contributing to heart disease complications.

Following diet plans which require you restricting carbs could lead to your body experiencing "Carb Flu" or "keto flu." This name is gotten from the ketogenic diet (which we will be discussing in the later stages of this book). More side effects of carb restriction are; Fatigue, Weakness, Nausea, Dizziness, Depression, etc.

As we have seen, eating too little carbs is not good for our health. If we, however, eat too many carbs containing high calories, it is still equally injurious. Carbs are necessary for our meals, but moderation is key. Understanding this moderation isn't as complicated as it seems. The advisable way to do this is by keeping to the guidelines, which I recommend later on in this book.

FATS

A side from carbohydrates, another class of food which are blamed for weight gain is Fats. It is even more associated to weight gain than carbohydrates. According to Wikipedia, "In nutrition, biology, and chemistry, fat usually means any ester of fatty acids or a mixture of such compounds; most commonly those that occur in living beings or food."

Fat is mostly used as a bad word in the food world. Some time ago, and even currently in some places, many people recommend the limitation or even total avoidance of fat in your meals to prevent weight gain and certain health issues such as diabetes and heart diseases. However, this is not entirely correct, as not all fats are bad. Some are essential in lowering your cholesterol level and keeping you healthy. Therefore, some fat is needed in your diet.

More important functions that fats perform in the body are; supply of energy, providing warmth, building cells, protecting organs, assistance in the absorption of vitamins from foods, and making hormones that are important to the body.

There are different types of fats, and you will need to fully understand them to fully grasp some of my dietary advice.

The difference between the two is based on their structural formula. They include:

Saturated Fats: These are solid at room temperature because their carbon atoms are completely covered or saturated. A diet with an excess of this can increase your cholesterol, sometimes towards the harmful LDL cholesterol. Due to this, blockages in arteries and increase in the risk of heart disease. This type of fat is common in butter, poultry skin, red meat, whole milk, dairy products, and eggs.

Unsaturated Fats: this type of fat contains fewer hydrogen atoms bound to carbon atoms, making the fats liquid at room temperature. The main sources of these fats include; vegetables, nuts, and fish. Unsaturated fats are good for the heart and other parts; therefore, it is highly recommended that you replace saturated and trans fats with them.

Unsaturated fats are in two forms; Monounsaturated fats, which have a single chemical bond and are found in oils that are liquid at room temperature and solid when refrigerated. They are found in avocado, olive, Peanut oils, canola, almond, hazelnut, pecans, and other nuts.

On the other hand, polyunsaturated fats are found in foods like flaxseed, soybean, corn, sunflower, tuna, salmon, and all fatty fishes.

Trans Fats: They are mostly made in an industrial process, though they can also be found naturally in animal-based foods such as meat and milk. To make them industrially, hydrogen is added to liquid vegetable oils at room temperature, making them solid. This makes them last longer with a satisfying taste and texture. They are present in French fries and all other fried foods, cakes, biscuits, doughnuts, pies and other baked food, margarine, frozen pizza, and microwave popcorn.

Trans fats usually taste good, but they are not so good for you. It is quite unhealthy as it raises your LDL cholesterol level, increasing your risk of heart disease, type 2 diabetes, and stroke. Sometimes, trans-fat-free foods are thought to be healthy, but this is not always the case as there might still be a lot of unhealthy saturated fats and other ingredients packed in them. Therefore, I will advise that you carefully read labels before you buy or eat any packaged food.

Generally, it is recommended by the American Heart Association themselves that nothing more than 5 – 6% of your daily calories should come from saturated fats. This means that if you are to eat 2,000 calories a day, ensure that only about 120 calories are gotten from saturated fats. The association also recommends that nothing more than 1% of your daily calories should come from trans-fat. Some places have even banned trans-fat in general.

What you use in place of saturated fats is very important. For instance, consuming polyunsaturated fat instead of saturated fats might decrease your heart disease, but using carbohydrates instead might increase the risk. In essence, this means that you should get most of your fats from unsaturated sources for the health of your heart and your general body. The major part of your nutrition, in general, should also be from healthy foods with low fats like fruits, vegetables, whole grain and lean protein like fish and skinless poultry.

Like carbohydrates, fats are not bad at all, but you just need the right balance between them and other nutrients. It would be best if you eat the healthiest types of fats and in the right amount. As a final tip, know that unsaturated fats are very healthy for you, whereas saturated and trans fats are not too good.

Fats are stored mostly in the human body subcutaneously (or under the skin. This layer of fat under the skin is composed of fat cells. There are about 20 – 27 billion fat cells in the body of a thin adult person, while someone with much weight usually has anywhere between 75 to 300 billion.

Both genders do not store fat in the same places in the body. Females usually have subcutaneous fat in the breasts, waists, hips and buttocks. While in men, they can be found in the chest, abdomen, and buttocks. This is also the reason why women usually have bigger hips and men bigger stomachs.

Also, vital organs like kindness and the liver have some fat stored around them. Muscles are not left out as well, as fat is stored even in them. For a fact, fat storages within the muscles are increased as people get older. Also, if a person is to become more inactive, their muscles begin to shrink, and fats come in to replace them.

Fats are stored mainly as a source of energy for emergencies at a later date. These fats come in handy whenever a certain muscle needs more power. In this situation, enzymes are sent to a fat cell and break down its content; glycerol and fatty acids are then released into the bloodstream. This is then transported to the target muscle to supply the needed energy. However, the muscles hold on to these fats, converting them to get the energy they need.

The storage of fat in some places can be very frustrating and could even lead to self-consciousness. Certain locations are known for the storage of fat in higher quantities than others, and reducing or melting away these fats require some activities. But before we delve into it, it is important we know the various places where these fats are most commonly stored.

Stomach: This is the most popular region where fat is found in excess. Although men tend to store fats in this area more than women, the stored fat always packs around vital organs inside the body, which is a problem regardless of gender. This heightens the risk of suffering conditions such as high blood pressure, high triglycerides, type 2 diabetes and sleeps apnea. Abdominal fats that are found deep are called visceral fat.

Hips, Butt and Thighs: These parts are popular fat storage centers for women in general and are found a lot more in them than in men. Having this fat in excess cannot cause as huge damage as stomach fat. This is because it a subcutaneous, lying under the skin. People with this fat in excess in the lower body are usually referred to as having a pear-shape, while those who have it in excess in the upper body region are of an apple shape. If the fat is to be found near the upper thighs, specifically by the hips' sides, it is famously referred to using the slang term "saddlebags."

Calves: They are situated right below knees on the back of the legs and are made up of the gastrocnemius and soleus muscles. These locations are also favorites of fats, most especially when they are not toned. It is most often referred to as cankles, meaning having fat by the calves and ankles.

Underarms: These are where the famous three-part muscles, the triceps, are found. When well-toned or developed, they usually have a horseshoe shape. But when otherwise, fat begins to store there. Also, more fat can be stored close to it, in the armpit area.

Back: This is another site where fats are stored irrespective of gender. Fats are stored equally in the upper and lower areas. When found in women's upper parts, it is commonly referred to as "bra overhang."

Sides: The abdomen's sides are known to contain muscles called obliques shaped diagonally and aid the rotating and twisting of the torso. Fats also build over these muscles regularly, and this is famously called "love handles."

Chest: The muscles in the chest of both genders are known as the pectorals. However, fats begin to store here, mostly in men's bodies, when they do not exercise or develop their muscles. This causes flabbiness that is usually called man breasts, moobs, or man boobs.

In conclusion, if you are looking to lose some weight, you should not use this chapter as an excuse to give up. Because while you can't completely control your body's working, you can always learn how to beat weight gain through controlling your eating habits and changing your lifestyle. So, unless you have an unavoidable medical condition opposing you, you have all it takes to control your weight, and you will learn all about it shortly.

Introduction To Weight Loss

In Medicine, health or physical fitness, weight loss refers to reduction in the total body mass. This includes loss of body fat, fluids, mineral deposits, muscles, etc. It occurs both intentionally and unintentionally. In the latter, it could be as a result of malnourishment or an underlying disease. While in the former, it is mainly a conscious attempt to reduce one's weight.

It is very natural for anyone to make efforts to lose weight as quickly as possible. However, those who lose weight gradually are more successful when it comes to keeping this weight off. Healthy weight loss requires a program containing *diet, exercise, and change in general lifestyle.*

Losing weight is not always easy; it will take a commitment on your part, and every other thing is provided in this guide. Also, you should have it in mind that even losing weight only modestly can be very beneficial to you. It could produce health benefits like gradually improving your blood pressure, cholesterol, and sugar levels. For example, if your weight drops by 5% from 200 to 190 pounds, you may still be classified under the overweight or obese range, but the modest loss in weight will still decrease your risk factors for obesity-related diseases. Therefore, even if your goal is to lose a lot more weight than you have already lost, it's best you see it as a journey or a gradual process with your final destination in mind. Another benefit you stand to gain is that you will learn new habits (both eating and physical ability), making your lifestyle healthier. These habits will continue to help you maintain your lost weight even for a lifetime.

According to the National Weight Control Registry study, individuals who achieved significant weight loss had noticeable improvements in physical health, energy levels, physical mobility, general mood, and self-confidence.

When it comes to losing weight, people usually come up with many excuses. A good number just lack the motivation needed to achieve their body goals. Below are the three general reasons why you should lose weight. They may also serve as more motivation for you.

General Appearance: Although many people aren't satisfied with how they look, others just act like they are and may want to urge you to do the same but are not genuinely happy themselves. If you are overweight and unhappy with how you look, then your best bet is weight loss. In fact, this can turn out to be one of the best types of motivation you can give yourself. While losing weight, making notable progress can play a big role in improving your general appearance.

Overall Health: As we have seen in the earlier parts of this chapter, being overweight or obese has physical disadvantages like restricting your motion. It has been established that it is related to a good number of deadly diseases. Therefore, you should consider losing some weight for your own overall health benefits.

Mental Well-being and Stability: Besides benefiting your general appearance and overall health, weight loss can make you feel better about yourself. Losing a few weight will definitely increase your self-esteem and self-confidence. When put in the right mindset, you can overcome other issues you might have been struggling with.

Are you bothered with your body fats? Or are you worried if you would ever lose those stubborn fats? Just know that you are not alone, as many others are also faced with this issue across the country and even globally. If you are interested in losing your current weight, it may be easier said than done, but you can do it. And it's as easy as the guides I will give to you in the next chapter.

DIETARY PRESCRIPTION

We all have different bodies, with no two persons having exact types, not even twins. However, it is a fact that all our bodies, irrespective of a person's body form, need fuel to run. This fuel is gotten from the food we eat.

Eating carbohydrates (a major source of the fuel our body needs) is beneficial but may cause weight gain. However, there are ways to fuel our body system, carbohydrates or no carbohydrates.

In this chapter, we will focus on dietary prescription as a method of losing weight. This is just a process of deciding the type of food you eat, which can contribute significantly to your slimming down. For this study, we will be focusing more on the best two dietary prescriptions; Keto Diet and Green Smoothie. Let's begin!

KETO DIET

A ketogenic diet, or keto diet for short, is a controlled diet regimen that derives a major part of its calories from fat and only a little proportion from carbohydrates. This works on the body by forcing it to burn fats instead of carbohydrates for energy.

Normally, when you eat carbohydrates, they are converted to glucose to power the body and the brain. However, if you choose not to eat enough carbohydrates, the body uses fats as backup energy by converting the stored fat into the required energy.

Opting to go for a Ketogenic diet is like getting into a happy marriage. It is a commitment that gives you far more than it takes away. It may stop you from eating excess sugar, which a good number of us so love, but in return, you get better health, much more energy, a slimmer, trimmer body, and most importantly, the perfect body you've always dreamed of.

Without a doubt, one of the proven and best ways of reducing body weight and excess fat is through a Ketogenic diet. It was initially designed for seizures, but it has turned out to offer a lot more benefits to all humans. It is also widely accepted as it has been tested and is trusted by many scientists worldwide.

There are cogent things to keep in mind to get started on your Keto diets, and one of the necessities is the ingredients. I have done extensive research on proven keto diet ingredients that you can bank on to improve your body system and relieve you of those stubborn fats. Below is a detailed list of keto-friendly ingredients:

- **Vegetables:** All types of lettuce, greens such as collard, kale, mustard greens, turnip, spinach, Swiss chard, onion, garlic, mushrooms, squash, radishes, asparagus, broccoli, celery, eggplant, tomatoes, arugula, kohlrabi. The following should be moderation; cauliflower, fennel, green beans, artichokes, snow peas, okra, cabbage, and cucumbers.

- **Fruits:** Cranberries, lemon, raspberries, coconut, lime, lemon, and blackberries.

- **Meat and Poultry:** Beef, game, chicken, turkey, duck, lamb, pork, and veal.

- **Ground meat:** Turkey, pork, beef, and mixed ground meat.

- **Lunch and Deli Meats:** Pancetta, salami, prosciutto, speck, ham, pastrami, chorizo, bacon, and pepperoni. Bologna and mortadella should be in moderation.

- **Seafood:** Whitefish, crab, octopus, oysters, squid, scallops, lobster, mussels, and fatty fish.

- **Dairy:** Cream cheese, goat, blue cheese, mozzarella, brie, Gouda, camembert, heavy cream, butter, eggs, double cream, and provolone. The following should be moderate; whole milk, full-fat Greek yogurt, mascarpone, feta, pepper jack cheese, cheddar cheese, sour cream, ricotta, and cottage cheese.

- **Nuts and Seeds:** Peanuts, pine nuts, chia seeds, hemp seeds, pumpkin seeds, sunflower seeds, Brazil nuts, pecans, hazelnuts, and almonds.

- **Fats and Oils:** Coconut oil, flaxseed oil, cocoa butter, avocado oil, olive oil, nut oil, duck fat, lard, schmaltz, and tallow.

- **Drinks Options:** Zero carb energy drinks, keto smoothies, diet soda, coffee, tea, seltzer, and sparkling water.

- **Herbs and Spices:** Bouillon cubes and granules. They can either be fresh or dried.

- **Sauces and Condiments:** Mayonnaise, vinegar, mustard, tomato sauce, and hot sauce

- **Canned Food:** Crab, tomato, salmon, pickles, tuna anchovies, and olives.

- **Baking Ingredients:** Baking powder, cocoa, baking soda, vanilla extra, coconut flour, almond flour, dark chocolate.

- **Nut and Seed Butters:** Almond butter, peanut butter, pecan butter, coconut butter, walnut butter, tahini, macadamia nut butter, sunflower seed butter, and hazelnut butter.

- **Alcohol:** Whiskey, Brandy, vodka, tequila, and a dry martini.

- **Seaweed:** Nori, dulse, kelp, spirulina, and wakame.

- **Sweeteners:** Stevia drops, Splenda, erythritol, xylitol, monk fruit.

- When on a ketogenic diet, you do not consume everything. There are many things you should avoid. And below is the list of foods you are to avoid when on a ketogenic diet.

- **Grains and Grain-like seeds:** Wheat, oats, rice, barley, millet, corn, buckwheat, quinoa, and amaranth.

- **Flours:** Cornmeal, cassava, dal, fava beans, cornstarch, and wheat flour.

- **Starches:** soy, sago, banana, mesquite, plantain, lentils, tapioca, and starchy vegetables.

- **Sugars:** Avoid all types of sugar and syrup

- Processed vegetables and trans fat

- Milk and reduced-fat dairy products

- Factory farmed fish and eggs, processed meat

- Fruits other than berries and dried fruits sugary drinks

So that you do not waste money getting unnecessary things; stick to the list I have provided above.

Vital Keto Diet Tips

Before we go into various keto diets, here are some of the crucial things you should have in mind when using a keto diet.

Always Have a Solid Breakfast: Breakfast is known as the most important meal of the day. Even when on a keto diet, it is still as important. Therefore, you should look to starting your day well. When you have a healthy breakfast with the right amount of protein and fats like egg muffins, your q1 eating habit throughout your day will be controlled. Also, if you eat a healthy low-carb breakfast, your body's glucose levels are significantly restored, which is as important as fuel to a car. Make sure most of your breakfast contains foods rich in protein. Examples of these foods are seeds, nuts, milk, and eggs.

If you are to skip this breakfast for any reason, your cognitive function and mood will be affected. It may ultimately even lead to high cholesterol, hypertension, and high blood pressure. In fact, individuals who skip breakfast mostly have increase levels of fatigue all through the day. Skipping it often is even much worse.

Breakfast is a significant factor in having a successful keto diet and in bettering health in general. This is why I will give you just the right keto recipes later on to make easy breakfast prep a habit. Remember that your body needs instant refuel in the morning despite your weight, and you should therefore ensure your breakfast is taken within an hour of waking up.

Build Your Muscles: To have a successful keto diet, you will have to build lean mass gradually. This is very crucial as it will help you burn outstubborn fat storage in the body more efficiently. You can do many exercises to boost muscle size, and I have included them in the sixth chapter of this guide.

The building of muscles and keto diet complement each other to give improved athletic performance and help you lose weight in the best way possible.

Make Good Use of Nutrition Facts on Labels: Before you consume any product, make sure you check its nutrition facts label or table. This can help you make excellent and well-informed decisions.

It is important always to make sure that our meals are low on carbs. Aside from the health benefit it has, it will also help you make good meal choices that canadd value to your diet.

The Keto diet's worse enemy are added sugars. Unfortunately, most processed food contains hidden sugar and other sweeteners, which help preserve them. In fact, an average American consumes more than 64 pounds of added sugar every year; this is at an average of 22 teaspoons daily.

Added sugars and sweeteners are terrible for you if you are on a keto diet, as it disrupts everything. They add absolutely zero healthy value to your body. Always check the nutritional facts label and see if any of these ingredients are among; caramel, dextrin, cane juice solids, dextran, cane juice, beet sugar, , barley malt, golden syrup, buttered syrup, carob syrup, diastase, diastatic malt, Refiner's syrup, date sugar, and ethyl maltol.

If you must use a sweetener for your keto diet, choose a healthy sweetener that contains only natural ingredients without any chemicals. Examples of natural sweeteners that have health benefits are monk fruit and Stevia. Stevia is, in fact, 300 times sweeter than sugar and does not affect your system sugar level. If you need this, purchase a verified organic product. Another alternative is monk fruit, which has sweetener with zero-calorie and they have significant antioxidant and anti-inflammatory properties. Aside from generally being a good sweetener, itregulates insulin tolerance and reduces inflammation.

Be Aware of Net Carbs Consumption: Although it may be really confusing to pinpoint the exact amount of carbs you need in your daily meal, learning to calculate the net carbs you need to consume is crucial to having a successful keto diet. The most basic way to explain net carbs is simply the amount of carbohydrates that your body can breakdown and use effectively for energy generation. In calculating the net carbs in your keto diet, you should subtract the dietary fiber and sugar alcohols in grams from the total carbohydrate.

Your dietary fiber and most of your sugar alcohol are not digestible by your liver, and therefore, only count as starches and sugar. Calculating your net carbs can be a significant factor in your keto diet and should not be taken for granted. If you do not understand how to calculate it, I highly recommend that you research more on how to do so.

Eat Real Whole Foods: When most people say they are on a diet, they tend to avoid whole foods, thinking it benefits them. However, on a keto diet, it is key that you eat whole and unprocessed food with high nutrients. It will be in your advantage tostay far from junk food and chemical additives. Rather, you should focus only onorganic, nutritious, and wholefoods that will make youhealthier.

Take Note of the Energy Density: The energy density is just the amount of calories in each gram of your food. Eating moderate energy density food is important when on a keto diet, while high-density foods should be eaten in little amounts.

Lower density foods contain smaller amounts of calories in 1-gram of our foods and shouldn't be eaten too much as well. These include simple green salads with high water quantity, clear soups, and vegetables.

When hoping on a ketogenic diet journey, you should be expecting ideal weight loss as your body fats are burnt up when you avoid carbohydrates. You will also experience a significantly decreased appetite as well as higher energy levels.

In addition to this, your brain makes increased use of ketones as its main fuel source, consequently reducing toxins levels, thereby increasing mental clarity, focus, concentration, and mental performance in general. Lastly, due to the type of ingredients and nutrients involved, your body gains significant health benefits as well. With all that said, let us now go into the best foods you can eat in a ketogenic diet.

BREAKFAST DIETS

As we have explained earlier, breakfast is the most important meal of your day, and it is never a good idea to start your day hungry. With these easy to prepare breakfast recipes for a healthy keto diet, you can easily keep your carbs checked while being full all morning.

Ingredients

- Tablespoon of olive oil (1)
- Slices of bacon (7)
- Chopped red bell pepper (1)
- Heavy cream (½ cup)
- Grated Parmesan cream (¼ cup)
- Eggs (9)
- Salt and pepper
- Tablespoons of chopped parsley (2)
- Large Bella mushrooms (4)
- Chopped basil (¼ cup)
- Cubed mozzarella cheese (4 ounces)
- Chopped Goat cheese (2 ounces)

Steps

- Pre-set your oven to 350°F, then put your olive oil in a skillet, heat, add bacon and cook for about 5 minutes.
- Add in red pepper, cook for 2 minutes until it gets soft.
- Add cream, Parmesan cheese, eggs, parsley, salt and pepper to a bowl and mix.
- Add mushroom to your pot, stir and cook for 5 minutes. Add basil and cook for a minute. Add your mozzarella.
- Add in a mixture of egg, move ingredients about such that the egg sinks to the bottom. Add in goat cheese
- Place in oven for 8 minutes, then broil for 6 minutes.
- Use a knife to pry the frittata edges from the pan.
- Place on a plate and slice.

Nutrients: •*Calories   408* •*Total fats   31.2g*   •*Net carbs   2.4g*
•*Protein – 19.2g*   •*Fiber – 0.8g.*

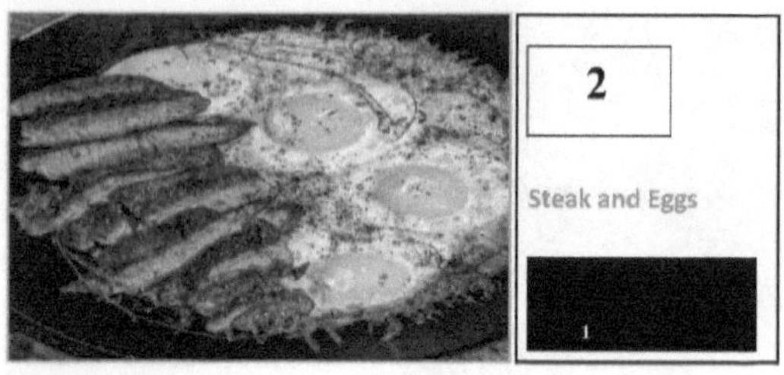

Ingredients

- Eggs (3)
- Tablespoon of Butter (1)
- Ounces of Sirloin (4)
- An Avocado (¼ of it)
- Salt
- Pepper

Steps

- Melt in your pan
- Fry the eggs until the whites have been set, and the yolk is done to your desired preference.
- Season with salt and pepper.
- Cook sirloin in a separate pan to your taste.
- Slice it into small strips and season with salt and pepper.
- Slice the avocado and add to your dish.

Nutrients: •Calories – 510   •Total fats – 26g   •Net carbs – 3g
•Protein 44g   •Fiber 0.

Ingredients

- Pieces of chicken sausage (1½)
- Teaspoons of rosemary (¼)
- Teaspoons of baking soda (⅛)
- Cup of Coconut flour (¼)
- Teaspoons of cayenne pepper (⅛)
- Teaspoons of salt (⅛)
- Egg yolks (5)
- Teaspoons of Lemon juice (2)
- Cup of Coconut oil (¼)
- Tablespoons of coconut milk (2)
- Grated Cheddar cheese (¾)

Steps

- Set oven to 350 F
- Chop sausage, while heating skillet
- Cook the sausage
- While the sausage is cooking, put all dry ingredients in a bowl, then mix egg yolks, lemon juice, coconut milk and oil in a separate bowl.
- Add the liquid to the dry mixture, add half cup of cheese, fold to combine, and put it into 2 ramekins.
- Add cooked sausages to the batter and push it in with a spoon.
- Bake for about 25 minutes (until top turns golden)
- Add the leftover cheese and broil for about 4mins.
- Serve warm

Nutrients:•Calories – 711   •Total fats – 65.3g   •Net carbs – 5.8g
          •Protein   34.3g   •Fiber   11.5g

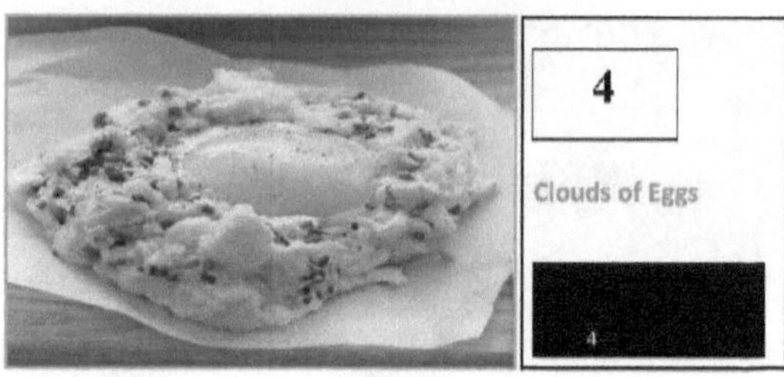

Ingredients

- Large Eggs (4)
- Slices of Bacon (2)
- Tablespoons of Parmesan cheese (2)
- Salt
- Pepper
- Onion powder
- Garlic powder

Steps

- Separate egg yolks from white.
- Cut up bacon into bits and cook.
- Pour eggs into a bowl and whip until stiff.
- Shred parmesan cheese into egg whites
- Add bacon bits.
- Separate egg white into four mounds on a silicon mat.
- Bake egg whites for 5 minutes at about 350° until they are set.
- Pour egg yolk into each mounds.
- Bake egg whites until brown.

Nutrients: •Calories 98 •Total fats 7g •Net carbs 1g
•Protein – 6g •Fiber – 0g.

Ingredients

- Cup of Almond Milk (1)
- Tablespoon of cacao powder (1)
- Tablespoons of Chia Seeds (1)
- Cup of Raspberry (¼)
- Agave or Xylitol (1)

Steps

- Combine almond milk and cocoa powder in a bowl and stir
- Add chia seeds and allow to rest for 5mins
- Use a fork to fluff the chia and cacao mixture
- Place in fridge and allow to chill for 30 minutes.
- Serve with raspberries and a drizzle of agave on top

Nutrients: •*Calories – 230*   •*Total fats – 20g*   •*Net carbs – 4g*
•*Protein   15g*   •*Fiber   0g.*

Ingredients

- Large eggs (4)
- Slices of Bacon (8)
- Tablespoon of Butter (1)
- Cup of chopped cauliflower or broccoli (½)
- Cup of finely chopped celery (⅓)
- Peeled carrot (1)
- Cup of Shredded Colby Jack Cheese (½)
- Cup of a large chopped White Onion (½)

Steps

- Slice bacon across its grain into smaller strips.
- Melt butter in a large skillet and put over medium heat.
- Add bacon and vegetables
- Stir your vegetables and bacon in the butter after about 20mins.
- The bacon should crisp on its edges, and the vegetables should become caramelizing.
- Spread mixture over the skillet evenly.
- Make one well in each quarter of the skillet.
- Break an egg into each well.
- Cook eggs until nearly done and sprinkle cheese on top.
- Allow to cool until cheese melts, and eggs are done.

Nutrients: •Calories – 220   •Total fats – 23g   •Net carbs – 3.2g
•Protein 17g   •Fiber 0g.

Ingredients

- Teaspoons of organic butter (3)
- Cup of roughly chopped toasted walnuts (¾)
- Cup of roughly chopped toasted macadamia (¾)
- Cup of unsweetened coconut shreds (½)
- Tablespoon of stevia (½) (optional)
- Cups of almond milk (2)
- Teaspoon of salt (⅛)

Steps

- Melt butter in pot and place over medium heat.
- Add toasted nuts to pot and stir for 2 minutes.
- Add shredded coconut into the pot and stir continuously so the ingredients do not burn.
- Drizzle with stevia (optional)
- Pour milk into pot, add salt and stir again.
- Turn off heat and allow for 10 minutes, so the ingredients soak in the milk.

Nutrients: •Calories – 515   •Total fats – 50.3g   •Net carbs – 14.4g
•Protein 6.5g   •Fiber 7.3g.

Ingredients

- Eggs (6)
- Cup of sliced spinach (½)
- Slices of shaved nitrate-free turkey (6)
- Light Mozzarella cheese
- Tablespoons of red onion (2)
- Tablespoons of red pepper (3)
- Fresh pepper
- Salt
- Olive oil spray
- Fresh Basil (optional)

Steps

- Heat oven to 350° F
- Slice spinach, grate mozzarella cheese and prepare red onion and pepper.
- Get a nonstick muffin tin and spray with olive oil.
- Put the turkey in a muffin tin cup, ensuring it's resting on both the sides and bottom of your tin.
- Crack an egg and pour in newly made turkey cup, and repeat for each egg and a cup.
- Add in spinach, red pepper, cheese, and red onion on each egg.
- Season each egg with salt and fresh pepper. You can now add basil (if using).
- Put the tin into the oven and bake until eggs are all set, and their whites

Nutrients: •Calories – 95   •Total fats – 6g   •Net carbs – 2g
•Protein 9g   •Fiber 0g.

Ingredients

- Eggs (2)
- Slices of Bacon (3)

Steps

- Heat oil in deep-fryer to 375°F.
- Cook bacon.
- Pour eggs into a prep bowl.
- Slip egg into center of the fryer (do not just drop the egg into it. Try to slip it in near the surface).
- Use two spatulas to corral your egg into a ball.
- Fry for about 4 minutes or until bubbling stops.
- Drain on paper towels.
- Enjoy!

Nutrients. •Calories – 321   •Total fats – 24g   •Net carbs – 1g
•Protein 27g   •Fiber 0g.

LUNCH DIETS

For lunch, you also have a wide variety of meals to enjoy. Here are some of the ones I've handpicked to help you get the best lunch while on a keto diet.

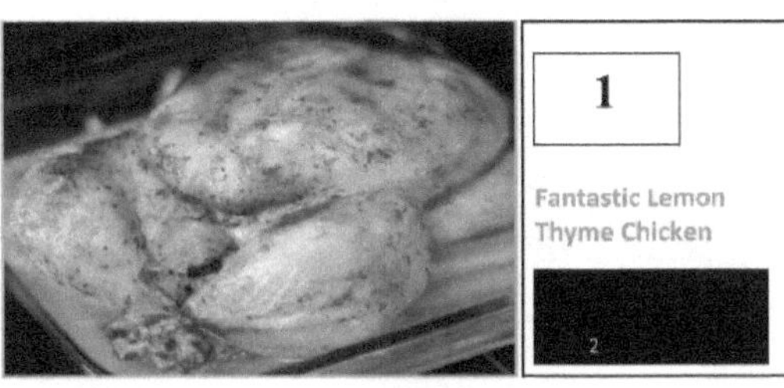

Ingredients

- Cloves of garlic (10-15)
- Sliced lemons (2)
- Ground pepper (½ teaspoon)
- Thyme (1 teaspoon)
- Whole chicken (3½ pounds)

Steps

- Arrange lemon and garlic on the base of a cooker
- Mix all spices together.
- Use spices to season the chicken
- Put seasoned chicken in the slow cooker.
- Cover and cook for 4 hours.
- Remove chicken and let it stand for 15 minutes.
- Enjoy!

Nutrients: •*Calories – 120*   •*Total fats – 8g*   •*Net carbs – 1g*
•*Protein   12g*   •*Fiber   0g*

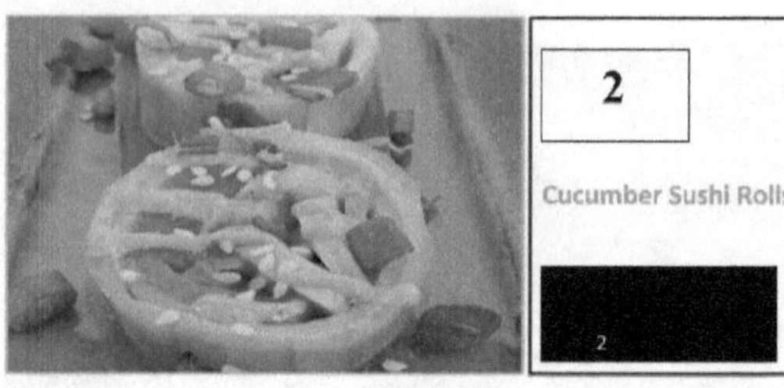

Ingredients

- Tuna Steak (½ pound)
- Cucumbers (2)
- Avocado (half of a whole)
- Shrimp (8)
- Mayonnaise(2 tablespoons)
- Sriracha (2 teaspoons)
- Sesame seeds (½ teaspoon)
- Green onions (1 stalk)

Steps

- Peel cucumbers and cut off ends
- Cut cucumbers to 6-8 inch long. Use wet long knife to cut into the cucumber.
- Mix mayonnaise and sriracha
- Take the end of cucumber with fish and roll onto itself. Ensure there are no air pockets and that the ingredients are sticking to themselves.
- Once you're almost done rolling (with about 3-4 inches left), spread some spicy mayonnaise on the cucumber and finish rolling. This helps seals the cucumber.
- Slice cucumber into ½ inch to 1 inch rounds. Hold both sides of the cucumber when slicing to maintain its shape.
- Chop green onions and sprinkle on top.
- Enjoy!

Nutrients: •*Calories – 322*   •*Total fats – 17g*   •*Net carbs – 25g*
•*Protein   36g*

3

Simple Chicken Salad

6

Ingredients

- Chicken breasts (4)
- Green peppers (105g)
- Celery (125g)
- Green onions (20g)
- Mayonnaise (¾ cup)
- Sugar-free sweet relish (¾ cup)
- Large hardboiled eggs (3)

Steps

- Heat oven to 350° F
- Add chicken to oven-safe pan
- Cook for about 45 – 60 minutes.
- Put 3 eggs in pan, fill with water, and boil.
- Once the water starts boiling (not the eggs), leave eggs for about 15 minutes.
- Chop onions, celery and pepper.
- When chicken is ready, bring out, allow to cool and chop.
- Combine all ingredients in a bowl.
- Chop eggs and mix in
- Split into 6 portions.
- Enjoy!

Nutrients:•*Calories – 413*   •*Total fats – 25g*   •*Net carbs – 2g*
          •*Protein   43g*

Ingredients

- Large eggs (3)
- Cream of tartar (¼ teaspoon)
- Cream cheese (3 ounces)
- Salt (¼ teaspoon)

Steps

- Preheat oven to 300°
- Separate eggs from egg yolks
- Beat egg whites until very bubbly.
- Add some tartar cream and beat until stiff peak is formed.
- Add 3 ounces of cream cheese and salt to egg yolk
- Beat mixture until yolks look pale yellow and have doubled size.
- Fold egg whites into yolk mixture
- Line cookie sheet with parchment paper.Spray oil or grease.
- Pour your batter as big as you want.
- Bake for about 30-40 minutes. Top of rolls are firm and golden when done.
- Leave on wire rack to cool.
- Enjoy!

Nutrients:•Calories – 48   •Total fats – 3.8g   •Net carbs – 0g
•Protein   2.3g

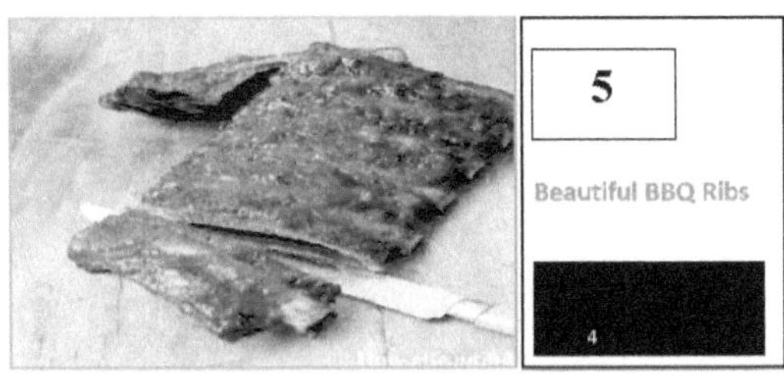

Ingredients

- Pork ribs (3 pounds)
- Olive oil (1 tablespoon)
- Tomato paste (1 can, 28 ounces)
- Hot water (½ can)
- Vinegar (½ can)
- Worcestershire sauce (6 tablespoons)
- Dry mustard (4 tablespoons)
- Chili powder (1 tablespoon)
- Ground cumin (1 teaspoon)
- Any powdered sweetener (1 teaspoon)
- Salt
- Pepper

Steps

- Heat olive oil in large frying pan
- Brown the ribs
- In aa separate bowl, combine the rest of the ingredients and mix thoroughly.
- Pour mixture on the ribs
- Cook for 8hours on low cooker.
- Serve and enjoy!

Nutrients.•Calories – 420   •*Total fats – 28g*   •*Net carbs – 14g*
•*Protein   38g*

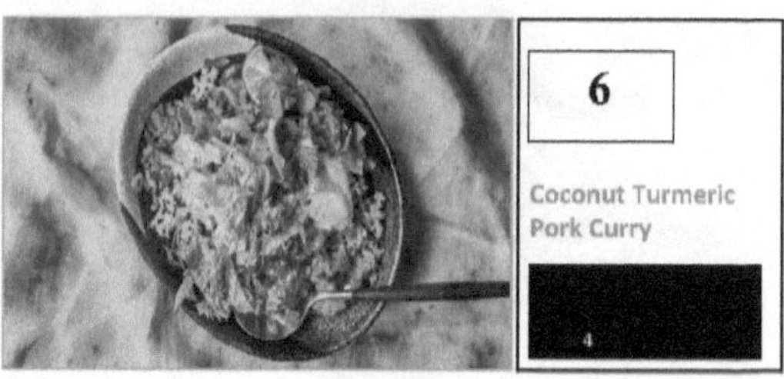

Ingredients

- Cubed pork shoulder (3 pounds)
- Coconut oil (1 tablespoon)
- Olive oil (1 tablespoon)
- Diced yellow onion (1)
- Minced garlic (2 cloves)
- Tomato paste (2 tablespoon)
- Coconut milk (1 can, 12 ounces)
- Water (1 cup)
- White wine (½ cup)
- Turmeric (1 teaspoon)
- Curry powder (1 teaspoon)
- Paprika (½ teaspoon)
- Salt
- Pepper

Steps

- Heat 1 tbsp of olive-oil in a saucepan.
- Sauté garlic and onions for 3 minutes
- Add pork and brown it
- Add tomato paste
- Mix remaining ingredients in a crockpot, and then add the pork
- Cover and allow to cook for 8hours on the low
- Divide into plates and enjoy!

Nutrients: •*Calories – 425*   •*Total fats – 31g*   •*Net carbs – 7g*
•*Protein   30g*

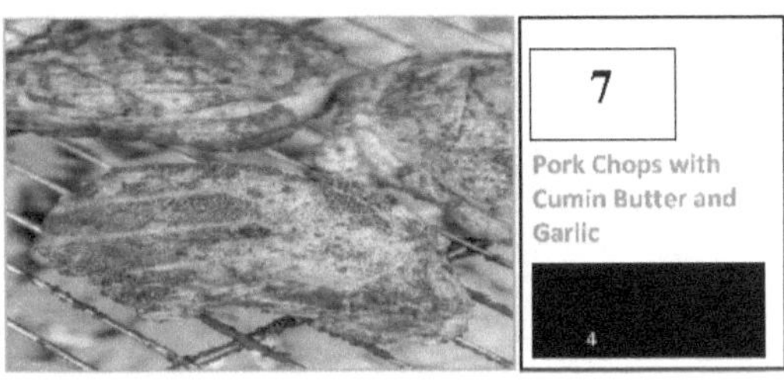

Ingredients

- Pork sirloin chops with the bone
- Salsa (½ cup)
- Butter (3 tablespoons)
- Lime juice (5 tablespoons)
- Ground cumin (½ tablespoon)
- Garlic powder (¾ tablespoon)
- Salt (¾ tablespoon)
- Black pepper (¾ tablespoon)

Steps

- Combine spices
- Season pork chops
- Melt butter in saucepan
- Sauce pork chops for 3 minutes on each side
- Place chops in slow cooker and pour salsa on it.
- Cover and cook for 3-4 hours.
- Serve and enjoy!

Nutrients:•Calories – 364   *•Total fats – 17g*   *•Net carbs – 3g*
•Protein   51g

Ingredients

- Smoked white fish (1 pound)
- Diced celery (¼ cup)
- Diced red onion (⅓ cup)
- Fraise crème (⅓ cup)
- Fresh chives (1 tablespoon)
- Fresh dill (1 tablespoon)
- Lemon juice (2 tablespoons)

Steps

- Place whitefish in bowl with onions and mix by tossing
- Combine crème fraise, cream cheese, dill and lemon in a separate bowl, and add pepper to desired taste
- Blend until creamy
- Add mixture to white fish and mix until blended.
- Refrigerate for 2hours.
- Serve and enjoy!

Nutrients: •*Calories – 386.7* •*Total fats – 12.2g* •*Net carbs – 4.2g* •*Protein 31g*

DINNER DIETS

Making dinner when on keto diets is often recommended, because even while your body rests, metabolism is still taking place. Therefore, you'll equally need healthy keto meals before you go to bed. The following are some of the best suitable for this.

Ingredients

- Chicken breasts (1 pound)
- Chicken broth (¾ cup)
- Lemon juice (1½ tablespoons)
- Sliced lemon (½ of a whole)
- Minced garlic (1 tablespoon)
- Basil (¼ teaspoon)
- Salt (½ teaspoon)
- Pepper (⅛ teaspoon)
- Garlic powder (¼ teaspoon)
- Oregano (¼ teaspoon)
- Melted butter (4 tablespoon)

Steps

- Mix all spices and melted butter together in a bowl
- Rub butter seasoning on both sides of chicken.Heat pan with butter
- Cook the seasoned chicken for about 7-10 minutes for both sides.
- Place chicken breast in a slow cooker and top with lemon slices
- Pour chicken broth in the cooker.
- Cover and cook for 6-7 hours of for 3-4 hours if heat is high.
- Serve and enjoy your dinner.

Nutrients:•Calories — 274   *•Total fats — 16.7g*   *•Net carbs — 3.4g*
•Protein — 26.9g

Ingredients

- Cream of celery or mushroom soup (½ can)
- Dry mix of onion soup (¼ packet)
- Beef for roasting (1 pound)

Steps

- Make some cut in the meat with a knife or fork.
- Place in crock-pot with fatty side facing up
- Add dry onion soup on top and on sides.
- Add the mushroom or celery soup.
- Spread meat on slow cooker, cover and cook for 3 hours on high.
- Remember to enjoy your dinner hot.

Nutrients •Calories – 280   •Total fats – 13.2g   •Net carbs – 2.5g
•Protein   35.5g

Ingredients

- Boneless and skinless chicken thighs cut into bit sizes (2 pounds)
- Pickled/canned jalapeños (2 ounces)
- Chopped small onion (1)
- Ground garlic (3 cloves)
- Ground cumin (1½ teaspoons)
- Chili powder
- Salt

Steps

- Set instant pot's cooking mode to "sauté".
- Coat chicken thighs with cumin, 1 teaspoon of chili powder and salt.
- Once the pot is hot, pour 3 teaspoons of oil into it.
- Add the pieces of coated chicken and allow to cook for 4-5 minutes.
- Add the remaining ingredients to the chicken and cover pot.
- Cook at high pressure settings for 15 minutes, and then natural pressure should be allowed to release for 10 minutes.
- Shred the chicken pieces more with a fork, and serve as tacos.
- Enjoy!

Nutrients:•Calories – 250
•Protein   15g
•Total fats – 5g
•Net carbs – g

Ingredients

- Unsalted butter (4 tablespoons)
- Diced onions (2)
- Boneless, skinless chicken breasts (2 pounds)
- 2 Pieces of ginger cut into ½ inch pieces.
- Garlic cloves (4)
- Sliced almonds (½ cup)
- Plain yoghurt (1 cup)
- Graham spice (2 teaspoons)
- Salt (1 teaspoon)
- Drained diced tomatoes (1 can)
- Heavy cream (¼ cup)

Steps

- Cut chicken breasts into 1-inch pieces
- Melt butter over flame
- Add onions and boil for 4-5 minutes
- Blend ginger, garlic, almonds, yogurt, graham spice and salt together until smooth
- Add tomatoes and combine with the mix.
- Put chicken at bottom of cooker, pour the tomato and mix.
- Cook on low for 4-5 hours.
- Enjoy while hot

Nutrients:•Calories –   *•Total fats – 19.4g*   *•Net carbs – 5.5g*
•Protein   37g

Ingredients

- Tomato paste (1 heaping tablespoon)
- Bone broth (1 cup)
- Sea salt and pepper
- Cumin (½ teaspoon)
- Ground beef (1 pound)
- Diced fresh parsley (small handful)
- Butter or ghee (2 tablespoons)
- Cauliflower (¼ large head)

Steps

- Mix meat with pepper, salt, paprika and cumin
- Make meat into 1-inch meatballs and put at the bottom of crockpot
- Mix paste and broth and pour over meatballs
- Set crockpot on high and cook for 2 hours.
- Chop cauliflower into flowers and steam until cooked.
- Mix water, salt, butter and pepper and blend until smooth.
- Put cauliflower mash into plate, add enough meatballs and sauce.
- Garnish with parsley and enjoy

Nutrients: •*Calories – 413*   •*Total fats – 17.4g*   •*Net carbs – 2.5g*
•*Protein 46.7g*

Ingredients

- Dark salad greens (6 cups)
- Walnut oil (¼ cup)
- Warm bacon grease (1 tablespoon)
- Apple cider vinegar (¼ cup)
- Fresh tarragon (1 tablespoon)
- Salt (½ teaspoon)
- Black pepper (½ teaspoon)
- Chopped walnuts (¼ cup)
- Chopped bacon (¼ cup)
- Goat cheese (¼ cup)
- Pomegranate seeds (1 tablespoon)

Steps

- Combine walnut oil, apple cider vinegar, tarragon, bacon grease, salt and black pepper in a bowl and blend well.
- Add salad greens to bowl and drizzle over them.
- Toss to coat.
- Add walnuts, bacon, goat cheese and pomegranate seeds.
- Mix and Serve.

Nutrients.•Calories – 259 •*Total fats – 4.9g* •*Net carbs – 3.5g*
•*Protein 5g*

Green Smoothie

Green smoothies are blends of fruits and vegetables which are highly rich in nutrients. They are quite popular for people looking to increase their intake of vitamins and minerals and are also a good way to facilitate weight loss.

The most basic form of making green smoothies is through the combination of leafy greens (such as kale, arugula, and spinach) and microgreens having a base liquid like water. You may be thinking these greens are very bitter, which of course, you'd be right. But this is true only when used alone, as you can always improve their flavor profile. However, adding more ingredients would only increase the amount of calories as sugar and fat content are increased. Fortunately, leafy greens are naturally low in these nutrients, but you are to make sure you're mindful to ensure your smoothie is balanced when you add these ingredients

There are many healthy additions to a green smoothie, and it depends solely on your preferences. You can add fruits or vegetables like apples, banana, mango, pineapple, avocado, carrot, cucumber, cauliflower, or beetroot. Other additions are nuts, seeds, herbs, spices, natural sweeteners, and some creamy additions (yogurt etc.).

Green smoothies are quite different from juicing (which we will look at later in this chapter), although they both have some basics. Making green smoothies require some laid down rules, and if done correctly, you can have an excellent means of weight loss by having your intake of calories cut down while enjoying what you ingest. Also, this method has been proven to be as effective as being on a keto diet itself.

When opting to go for green smoothies, all you need are just fresh greens and whatever fruits you prefer. I recommend that you combine about 6 parts of fruits with 4 parts of greens, but you can always start off with littler quantities of greens and increase later on. Another piece of advice is that you should have it in mind that some flavors are stronger than others and some fruits go better with certain kinds of vegetables. Therefore, you should keep an open mind and experiment with variations of combinations to see which is best for you.

Using this method for losing weight is usually done through fasting or alternatively by meal replacement. If you choose to fast, you will take in nothing else but your green smoothies for a week or two, before going back to your normal diet. It is a very quick and safe method of weight loss, but you should not fast for a long time. If you want to go on for longer periods of time, the best alternative is to take your green smoothie with your traditional meals but replacing one or two full meals. Breakfast is the preferable meal to replace as it is the best time for your body to take in these vital nutrients.

Green smoothies help ensure you live a very healthy and fit life for a long time, and in almost no time, I will provide you with some of the best recipes to carry on healthy life and, of course, lose weight. Now that I have given you a run-through of what green smoothies are, I will now give you some vital tips to set you on your way.

- Always buy organic products to avoid ingesting unhealthy chemicals.

- If your fruits are not organic, restrain from eating the peels. And always make sure to wash properly before eating.

- If your concoction tastes disgusting, add cucumber, lettuce, or celery to it. You can also add certain fruits such as apples and lemons.

- Alternate flavors so you don't end up drinking the same fruits and vegetables every time. This helps you go longer as you don't easily get tired of your diet, and so you get a wider range of nutrients.

- Research thoroughly before purchasing a juicer:

- Get something that meets your needs, so you don't end up wasting money.

- The softer and riper your fruits or vegetables, the thicker and richer in nutrients your juice will be.

- To get the best from leafy vegetables, roll them tightly into balls before feeding them to your juicer.

- Always clear up the pulp catcher frequently, as not doing so can make quite a huge mess over time.

- Feed-in the juiciest products last so it can clear up the pulp from the dryer ones.

- A blender can also function in place of your juicer.

- Leftover pulp can be used for stews or muffins.

- If you haven't gotten used to green smoothies, you can dilute your juice with filtered water, so you don't get stomach upset or diarrhea.

- Always clean up your juicer or blender after each use.

Green smoothies are extremely healthy and safe, and helps you in so many ways. Below are some of the best advantages you get from using this method.

It is a Good Method of Natural Weight Loss: The percentage of those who drink green smoothies and end up losing weight is so high that you can safely say just about anybody does after using this method. With green smoothies, your overall calorie intake is increased while vitamins, minerals and fiber are significantly increased. Your taste buds are also reset, helping you crave healthier foods.

Your Fruits and Vegetable Intake is Significantly Increased: According to the American Cancer Society, it is very important that you eat 5-9 servings of both fruits and vegetables daily as they help prevent cancer and other diseases. Green smoothies offer you a convenient way to take "bitter" vegetables while actually tasting fruits. Each green smoothie contains 3-5 or even more servings of fruits and vegetables.

It Provides Increased Energy: With green smoothies, you receive a powerful boost of vitamins, minerals, antioxidants and a lot more other nutrients without even having to fill up your digestive system. Since you are still eating whole foods and still fee light, you will receive much more energy to carry out your daily activities.

It is a Great and Genuine Way of Boosting Nutrition: Green smoothies are greatly packed with nutrients. For a fact, the right recipes of green smoothies can provide 100% of your daily quality amount of vitamins A, C and K, as well as an excellent source of all Vitamin Bs (except B12), vitamin E, and folate. You also get a great source of calcium, iron, magnesium, manganese, phosphorus, potassium, copper, and many other trace minerals. Green smoothies are the best way of receiving the nutritional values of salad, and their preparations are faster and a lot more convenient.

It Significantly Strengthens Your Immune System: With the good amount of Vitamins, Minerals, antioxidants and other compounds supplied by green smoothies, your immune system is well boosted, keeping you healthy for a long time. Ingredients such as cranberries, ginger and citrus fruits are extremely wonderful immune boosters.

A Great Source of Minerals For Healthier Bones: With green smoothies, you get a very rich source of minerals from the greens, alongside an abundant supply of calcium, magnesium and phosphorus. All these are the most important nutrients to facilitate bone building. Therefore, you can develop better, healthier and stronger bones.

BEST GREEN SMOOTHIES

Green Milk-Free Smoothies

1	Green Spinach and Lettuce Smoothie	Yield: 2 glasses

Ingredients

- Chopped romaine lettuce (3 cups/1 head)
- Chopped spinach leaves (2 cups/ half a large bunch)
- Sliced celery (½ cup)
- Diced apples (½ cup/ ½ of whole medium-sized)
- Diced pear (¼ cup/ 1 medium-sized)
- Sliced banana (½ cup)
- Fresh lemon juice (½ tablespoon)

Steps

- Thoroughly wash all vegetables and fruits.
- Put romaine lettuce, spinach and water all in a blender.
- Blend at low speed until mixture becomes smooth
- Add celery, apple and pear.
- Blend mixture at high speed.
- Add the banana and lemon juice and puree until well blended.
- Pour into glass and serve fresh.
- You can add ½ cup of parsley and cilantro each for greener smoothies.
- You can an inch of ginger to get an extra zing.

2 — Spinach and Collard Greens Smoothie

Yield: 1 glass

Ingredients

- Fresh spinach (1 cup)
- Fresh Collard greens (1 cup)
- Medium-sized oranges (4 whole)
- Pineapple chunks (3 cups)

Steps

- Squeeze out juice from oranges.
- Blend the spinach and collard greens together, using the fresh orange juice as liquid base.
- Blend at slow speed until smooth
- Add pineapples to the mixture and blend at high speed until it is well mixed.
- Pour and serve immediately

3 — Minty Papaya Green Smoothie

Yield: 1 glass

Ingredients

- Spinach leaves (3 cups)
- Cubed ripe papaya (2 cups)
- Cubed pear (1 cup)
- Fresh or dried goji berries (2 tablespoons)
- Fresh leaves of mint (fresh)

Steps

- Pour water into blender.
- Respectively add papaya, then the pear, berries, mint leaves and lastly spinach.
- You can blend for 30-seconds at high speed.
- Serve fresh
- You can replace papaya with an equal amount of banana.

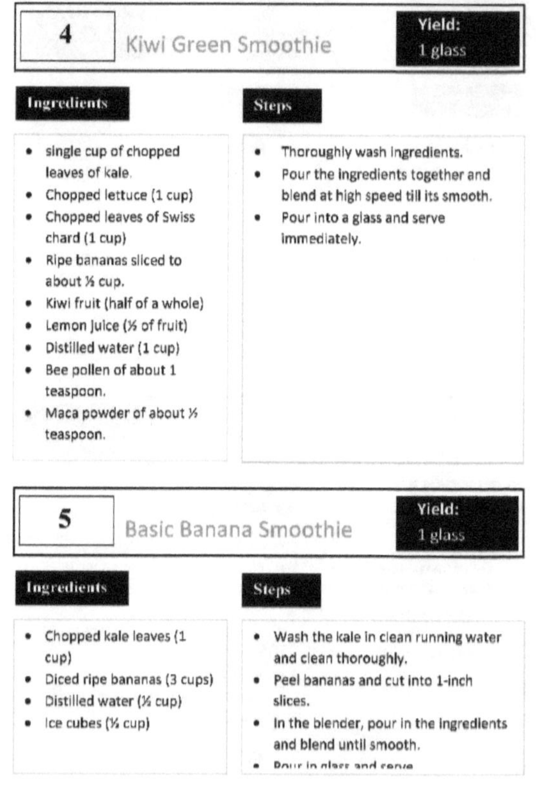

<table>
<tr><td>4</td><td>Kiwi Green Smoothie</td><td>Yield:
1 glass</td></tr>
</table>

Ingredients

- single cup of chopped leaves of kale.
- Chopped lettuce (1 cup)
- Chopped leaves of Swiss chard (1 cup)
- Ripe bananas sliced to about ½ cup.
- Kiwi fruit (half of a whole)
- Lemon juice (½ of fruit)
- Distilled water (1 cup)
- Bee pollen of about 1 teaspoon.
- Maca powder of about ½ teaspoon.

Steps

- Thoroughly wash ingredients.
- Pour the ingredients together and blend at high speed till its smooth.
- Pour into a glass and serve immediately.

<table>
<tr><td>5</td><td>Basic Banana Smoothie</td><td>Yield:
1 glass</td></tr>
</table>

Ingredients

- Chopped kale leaves (1 cup)
- Diced ripe bananas (3 cups)
- Distilled water (½ cup)
- Ice cubes (¼ cup)

Steps

- Wash the kale in clean running water and clean thoroughly.
- Peel bananas and cut into 1-inch slices.
- In the blender, pour in the ingredients and blend until smooth.
- Pour in glass and serve

| **6** | Green Chocolate Smoothie | **Yield:** 1 glass |

Ingredients

- Chopped kale leaves (½ cup)
- Chopped romaine lettuce leaves (1 cup)
- Swiss chard (¼ cup)
- Sliced ripe bananas (1 cup)
- Unsweetened cacao powder (1 teaspoon)
- Natural honey (1 tablespoon)

Steps

- Rinse and prepare all greens and fruits.
- Peel bananas and cut into 1-inch slices
- In the blender, pour in the ingredients and blend until smooth.
- Pour in glass and serve while fresh.

| **7** | Super Green Smoothie | **Yield:** 1 glass |

Ingredients

- Chopped kale leaves (1 cup)
- Brussels sprouts (½ cup)
- Spinach leaves (½ cup)
- Avocado (½ of a whole)
- Medium-sized green apple (1)
- Filtered water (½ cup)
- Ice cubes (½ cup)

Steps

- Wash and prepare all greens.
- Remove the flesh of the avocado, then discard the seed.
- Without peeling, core the apple and cut it into 1-inch cubes.
- Put kale, Brussels sprouts, spinach and filtered water in a blender and mix until smooth.
- Add avocado, apple and ice cubes and blend until smooth. Pour and enjoy!

8 — Summer Salad Smoothie:

Yield: 1 glass

Ingredients

- Leaves of mint (10)
- Leaves of sweet basil (10)
- Leaves of coriander (10)
- Watermelon chunks (2 cups)
- Small avocado fruit (½ of whole)
- Cucumber slices (¼ cup)
- Half lime fruit juice
- Distilled water (¼ cup)

Steps

- Remove all seeds from watermelon before cutting them into chunks.
- Scoop out flesh from avocado fruit.
- Slice cucumbers into half-inch thickness.
- Put mint first, then basil, coriander, water, watermelon, avocado, cucumber, and lastly lime juice, then blend on high speed until smooth.
- Pour into glass and enjoy.

9 — Apple Broccoli Detox Smoothie

Yield: 2 glasses

Ingredients

- Shredded romaine lettuce (1 cup)
- Broccoli heads (½ cup)
- Medium-sized apple (1)
- Half an orange
- Distilled water (½ cup)
- Ice cubes (1 cup)

Steps

- Properly rinse all greens with running water
- Peel and core apple, then cut it into 1-inch cubes.
- Peel orange, remove all seeds and separate into segments.
- In the blender, pour in the ingredients and blend at high speed until they are all properly mixed.
- Pour in a glass and enjoy.

<table>
<tr><td>10</td><td>Green Coconut Smoothie</td><td>Yield:
1 glass</td></tr>
</table>

Ingredients

- Chopped kale leaves (1 cup)
- Sliced ripe bananas (1 cup)
- Raw honey (1 teaspoon)
- Coconut meat (1 cup)
- Coconut water (1 cup)

Steps

- In the blender, pour in the ingredients and blend until smooth.
- Pour in a glass and serve immediately.

Green Milky Smoothies

If you prefer your smoothies molly, here are a few options for you.

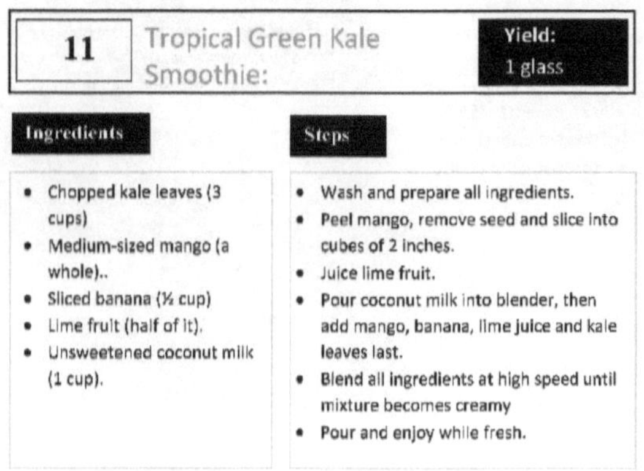

12 — Spinach Yogurt Smoothie

Yield: 2 glasses

Ingredients

- Chopped spinach leaves (2 cups)
- Large orange (1 whole)
- Sliced bananas (½ cup)
- Strawberries (⅓ cup)
- Plain yoghurt (⅓ cup)
- Ice cubes (1 cup)

Steps

- Peel orange and divide into segments. Remove seeds if any.
- In the blender, pour in the ingredients and puree until smooth.
- Pour in glass and enjoy immediately.

13 — Caramel Banana Green Smoothie

Yield: 2 glasses

Ingredients

- Spinach (1 cup)
- Sliced banana (1 cup)
- Store-bought caramel (1 cup)
- Walnuts (1 tablespoon)
- Coconut milk (¼ cup)
- Non-dairy milk (¼ cup)

Steps

- Put spinach, coconut milk and non-dairy milk into blender and blend until they are all well mixed.
- Add bananas, caramel and walnuts and blend until they become smooth.
- Pour in a glass and serve.

| 14 | Pineapple and Coconut Spinach Smoothie | Yield: 1 glass |

Ingredients

- Spinach (1 cup)
- Pineapple chunks (3 cups)
- Coconut milk (¼ cup)
- Water (½ cup)
- Ice cubes (½ cup)

Steps

- Pour all ingredients into a blender and blend until thoroughly mixed.
- Pour in a glass and enjoy.

| 15 | Peach Yogurt Green Smoothie | Yield: 1 glass |

Ingredients

- Spinach (1 cup)
- Small peaches (3 whole)
- Sesame seeds (1 tablespoon)
- Dried apricots (¼ cup)
- Non-diary milk (¼ cup)
- Non-diary yogurt (¼ cup)
- Ice cubes (½ cup)

Steps

- Put spinach, milk and yogurt together and blend until smooth.
- Add remaining ingredients and blend until thoroughly mixed.
- Pour in glass and enjoy.

Green Thick Smoothies

If your preference is a thick smoothie, the following are best for you.

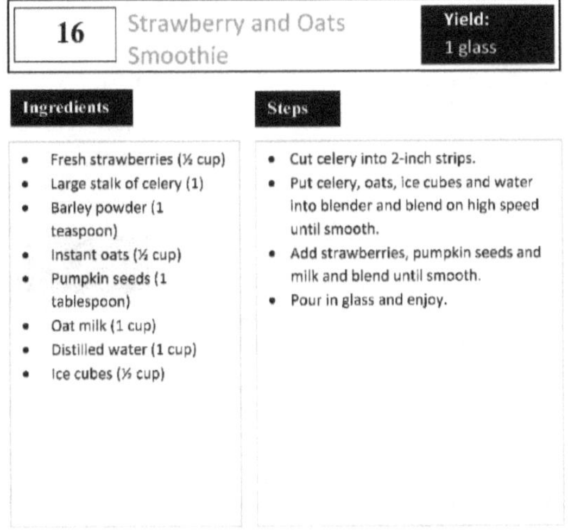

<table>
<tr><td>16</td><td>Strawberry and Oats Smoothie</td><td>Yield:
1 glass</td></tr>
</table>

Ingredients

- Fresh strawberries (½ cup)
- Large stalk of celery (1)
- Barley powder (1 teaspoon)
- Instant oats (¼ cup)
- Pumpkin seeds (1 tablespoon)
- Oat milk (1 cup)
- Distilled water (1 cup)
- Ice cubes (½ cup)

Steps

- Cut celery into 2-inch strips.
- Put celery, oats, ice cubes and water into blender and blend on high speed until smooth.
- Add strawberries, pumpkin seeds and milk and blend until smooth.
- Pour in glass and enjoy.

<table>
<tr><td>17</td><td>Broccoli and Blueberry Super Smoothie</td><td>Yield:
1 glass</td></tr>
</table>

Ingredients

- Broccoli (⅓ cup)
- Blueberries (½ cup)
- Sliced bananas (⅓ cup)
- Oats (¼ cup)
- Sunflower seeds (½ tablespoon)
- Non-dairy milk (½ cup)
- Water (¼ cup)
- Ice cubes (⅓ cup)

Steps

- Pour ice cubes, water, broccoli and oats in blender and blend on high speed until well mixed.
- Add milk, blueberries, bananas and sunflower seeds and blend until smooth.
- Pour in a glass and serve.

<table>
<tr><td>18</td><td>Orange Strawberry Dandelion Smoothie</td><td>Yield:
1 glass</td></tr>
</table>

Ingredients

- Dandelion leaves (1 cup)
- Orange juice squeezed from a medium-sized orange (¼ cup)
- Strawberries (2 cups)
- Pecan nuts (1 tablespoon)
- Dried pitted dates (½ cups)
- Oats (¼ cup)
- Ground vanilla (½ teaspoon)
- Cinnamon (½ teaspoon)
- Barley powder (½

Steps

- Put water, orange juice, strawberries and dandelion leaves in blender and blend until thoroughly mixed.
- Add the rest ingredients, and blend until smooth.
- Pour in glass and enjoy.

19 — Pistachio Ice Cream Kale Smoothie

Yield: 2 glasses

Ingredients

- Green kale leaves (1 cup)
- Diced ripe bananas (3 cups)
- Raw cashew nuts (½ cup)
- Maple syrup (1 tablespoon)
- Alcohol free pure vanilla extract (1 tablespoon)
- Chopped ginger (½ teaspoon)
- Filtered water (½ cup)
- Ice cubes (3 cups)
- A pinch of salt to taste

Steps

- Put all ingredients into a blender, putting all liquids first and greens last.
- Blend on high speed until mixture is smooth and creamy.
- Pour in glass and enjoy

20 — Green Muesli Smoothie

Yield: 1 glass

Ingredients

- Romaine lettuce (½ cup)
- Ripe mango chunks (½ cup)
- Diced ripe bananas (½ cup)
- Muesli (½ cup)
- Sesame seeds (1 tablespoon)
- Pitted dates (¼ cup)
- Non-diary milk (½ cup)
- Distilled water (½ cup)

Steps

- Put water, milk, muesli, and lettuce in blender, and mix well.
- Put in the rest ingredients, and blend until smooth.
- Pour in glass and enjoy.

Being fit and achieving an effective weight loss does not necessarily mean depriving yourself of essential nutrients and that joy of eating. The journey to weight loss is best embarked on by reducing your intake of calories while still taking in as many nutrients as you can. If followed correctly, the dietary prescription I have given you will be a potent tool in shedding pounds and keeping your health at an optimum level.

There are many other alternatives to gaining an effective weight loss, but you should definitely explore a more prescribed dietary mix here and there and say hello to a new, slimmer, and healthier lifestyle!

LIFESTYLE INTERVENTION

Aside from being on strict diets or making extra physical efforts to lose weight, it would be best to put some little things into consideration in your life to have that wholesome result you dreamt about.

In the simplest term, lifestyle intervention in weight loss is making changes in the way you live for the sole purpose of burning fats. These changes cover a wide range of activities, but we will only look at the specific and necessary things that needed to be done in this chapter.

MOTIVATION

It can be quite challenging to start a healthy weight loss plan and stick to it all through. Some people tend to lose focus and reason, hence quitting halfway through, while others just lack the drive even to begin.

To desire to lose weight and actually make an effort to achieve it, you will need a driving force to get you started and keep you going. This driving force here is motivation. Strong motivation is extremely important if you wish to change your lifestyle for weight loss. However, it is not something that just comes; you will have to seek it.

There are different ways to become motivated, it could be self-effected, meaning you get it yourself, or it could be done by the impact of people and the things around you. However, the main thing is self-motivation because you play the role of choosing to let any other thing affect you. It is only when you are self-motivated to a certain extent that you can gain any more motivation. Therefore, it is vital that you always boost your self-motivation and determination.

Before changing your lifestyle, you need first to change your mindset. The first way of doing this is by defining the reason you want a change of lifestyle. In this context, that is why you want to lose weight. You can even write them down to boost your motivation and commitment.

Make sure these reasons are for long-term success, so you do not end up returning to your old lifestyle, which could ultimately lead to you gaining your weight back. Remember that setting unattainable goals will only make you get frustrated and lose your resolve.

You can gain more motivation by choosing the right role models, joining supportive social groups or keeping supportive friends, having a positive mind among a host of other methods. In essence, consciously losing weight or making efforts to is impossible without motivation. Therefore, you should first make an effort to change your mindset before attempting to change your life.

LIFESTYLE STRATEGIES

True, almost everyone will love to shed off a few weight, especially those with much of it. However, most of the famous ways of losing weight come with little hurdles here and there. As we saw in the last chapter, going on diets is one of the most effective weight loss methods, but you may have to sacrifice a lot depending on the strength of your resolve. Fortunately, there are some simple changes to your lifestyle – or like I'll love to call it, lifestyle strategies – which can help you lose significant weight and keep it off. It's as easy as making simple tweaks to your lifestyle.

Below are some of the easiest ways to lose a good amount of weight without doing too much.

Eat Breakfast Everyday: One common mistake people make is thinking that skipping breakfast is a good way of cutting down their calories. However, this is very bad as it not only has health hazards, but it makes you eat a lot more during the day. In fact, people who eat breakfast usually have lower BMIs than those who skip breakfast, and they tend to perform even better. Therefore, always make sure you have a nutritious start to your day.

Close the Kitchen at Night: One common habit is eating late-night snacks and junk food, especially when watching

TV. This has become quite an addiction, and we have seen how much junk food disrupts weight loss. Therefore, you should set a time when you won't eat anything until the following day. Before long, you can get used to it, and it will significantly cut down your junk food consumption.

Be Careful When Choosing Your Liquid Calories: Avoid sweetened drinks. Most of them contain ingredients that pile up calories, and even worse, do not reduce much hunger. Replace sweetened drinks with water, citrus, low-fat milk or little portions of 100% fruit juice. You can also take vegetable juice or green smoothies if you get hungry in-between meals. Also, if you are used to taking alcohol most days, limit it to the weekends, and you can save yourself a handsome amount of calories.

Consume more Produce: According to the U.S. government's Dietary guidelines in 2005, the daily amount of produce adults should eat is about 7-13 cups. If you choose to eat more low-calorie fruits and vegetables, it can help you get over your cravings for foods high in fat and calories. Change your eating plan and include more fruits and vegetables, and you will definitely see progress in your weight loss.

Control Your Environments: Another simple lifestyle strategy is controlling your environment. To help cut down calories, you have to make your environment suitable for this purpose. Be careful in everything you do, like changing your stock of food to lots of healthier options, choosing the right restaurants and avoiding those that will tempt you to go against your resolve, the kind of places you go in general. The point is, avoid select suitable environments that'd support weight loss.

Be More Active, Add Extra Steps: Increase your activity rates, do whatever you can to be more active during the day. Consider getting a pedometer and add extra steps daily. Some famous healthy lifestyle habits to consider are walking short distances, going for walks regularly, pacing whenever bored, walking or riding a bike to work, running errands, taking the stairs instead of using the elevator, parking farther away from destinations and walking the remaining distances etc. Getting a pedometer can serve as a constant reminder and as motivation as well.

Switch to Lighter Alternatives: You can effortlessly trim calories by merely going for lighter products. Always go for low-fat alternatives when choosing salad dressings, dairy products, and every other product. Only doing this for the majority of your meals can be very effective in losing weight.

Yoga

Yoga, as a kind of exercise, has been in existence for thousands of years now. It focuses on strength, flexibility, and breathing, using them to boost individuals' physical and mental well-being.

Although its main components are exercises for strength and flexibility, and breathing, it has many advantages to many individuals. It combines a wide variety of physical postures, breathing techniques, and meditation which are collectively useful in solving many problems such as high blood pressure, heart diseases, aches and pains, stress, depression, and, as you must have already guessed right, over-weightiness.

In more recent years, yoga has expanded to every part of the world as a form of activity that promotes improved control of the mind and enhanced well-being on many levels. Despite the many ways in which yoga can be combined to help our lives in general, we will focus on how it can be beneficial to weight loss.

Yoga is vital in mindfulness. Its mental and spiritual benefits help individuals develop their mindfulness, increasing their awareness on many levels. This can boost your consciousness of how foods affect your mind, spirit, and, most importantly, your body.

Studies have proven that developing mindfulness through yoga can help people resist unhealthy foods much better. They also avoid overeating as they better understand their bodies, helping them notice when they're full.

Yoga practice prevents individuals from practicing it when full. This is especially important as it will help you make healthier food choices before practicing. It will also increase your likelihood of craving fresh, unprocessed food while encouraging less consumption.

All these are especially beneficial to people struggling with weight and want to lose some.

Yoga helps a great deal in burning calories. Although it is expected to be an aerobic exercise, various forms employ more physical efforts than others.

Active styles are very good at burning most calories, thereby preventing weight gain and facilitating weight loss. ***Ashtanga, vinyasa***, and ***power yoga*** are some important examples of yoga that are more of a physical nature. The last two, which are also offered in most hot yoga studios, keeps you moving almost constantly, thereby burning calories effectively.

Yoga facilitates metabolism. Aside from the physical part of yoga, the restorative part, which is less physical, also helps in weight loss. This type is especially useful in reducing abdominal fat and is very promising for people whose body weight serves as an obstruction to performing more vigorous yoga forms.

To effectively lose weight, it is advisory to practice yoga as often as possible. Intense practices should be done for an hour or more for at least 3-5 times weekly. While on other days, you should practice more relaxing forms like the restorative yoga.

As a beginner, do not rush into more complex forms. Instead, you should start slowly and gradually and build up. With this, you can build up strength and flexibility while preventing injuries. For days you may not complete full classes; simply carry out self-practice for about 20 minutes. Also, it is key that you rest for a full day a week.

For best results, yoga practices shouldn't be done alone but should be combined with physical activities like walking, cycling or swimming. This also benefits the individual by adding cardiovascular improvements. Also, weighing shouldn't be done after each practice, as it can be inaccurate since water weight can be temporarily lost.

Registering for full yoga sessions or classes can be very beneficial in losing weight. Alternatively, below are some of the best yoga poses you do at home.

Sun Salutations

Sun salutations are very effective for burning calories and increasing lean muscle mass. This helps in improving metabolism, thereby facilitating weight loss.

When practicing, to get the best results, reps should be at least 10. Intensity, if preferred, can be increased by holding some positions for much longer periods or by increasing the pace.

How to do it:

- Stand, lift your arms over your head, inhaling as you do so.
- Swan dive downwards to a forward bend and exhale at the same time.
- Move your feet back into the plank pose.
- Hold the position for at least 5 breaths.
- Dropdown your knees, lowering your body to the floor.
- Extend legs, turn feet tops to the mat, and place your hands under your shoulders.
- Lift partway, halfway, or all the way into Cobra pose while inhaling during any of the processes.
- Lower back down, exhaling, and push into a Downward Facing Dog.
- Hold the pose for about 5 breaths.
- Move feet to the top of mat, and stand in a Forward-Bend while exhaling through.

- Inhale while lifting up your arms over your head.
- Lower your arms back down, exhaling.

- **Boat Pose**

This is a pose reputed for engaging all your body, your core most especially. It is key mostly for the reduction of stress, strengthening abdominals, hip flexors and spine. It also stimulates the kidney, prostate, thyroid and intestines, thereby improving digestion.

How to do it:

- Sit on the floor, put your legs together, and extend them in front of you.
- Bend your knees and lift your feet off the floor. Your thighs should be at am angle to the floor, and your shins parallel to the floor.
- Extend arms in front of you, putting them parallel to the floor.
- Try to straighten your legs while your torso is kept lifted.
- Hold pose for 30 seconds.
- Repeat for about 5 times.

- **Plank Pose**

This is seen as one of the best methods of burning calories. This pose engages multiple muscles simultaneously, making it very beneficial to the core of the body. The plank pose is vital for improving posture, flexibility, and, importantly, weight loss. For best results, the pose should be done for a total of 10-20 minutes.

- Attain tabletop position, and step feet back while heels are lifted.
- Bring your body to a straight line, if possible, in front of a mirror.
- The core, arm and leg muscles should all be engaged.
- Hold this pose for about a minute.

Remember to always stick to what you can do. Start with easier procedures, and make gradual improvements. If you want are more detailed explanation of the practices as mentioned above, watch tutorial videos to better your understanding.

In conclusion, aside from making a physical effort to shed off weight, when your awareness and practice in general are deepened, you become more naturally attracted to healthy foods and better living ways in general.

Exercise Solutions For Weight Loss

An exercise is any physical activity aimed at conditioning parts of the body for improving health and maintaining fitness. It is an exercise only when well structured, repetitive, and most importantly, planned. It is also regularly related to sweat, heavier breathing, and an increase in heart rate.

A workout is a session of related exercises following a specific pattern, which improves fitness. Many people usually mix up exercises and workouts due to their similar nature. However, exercise is a more general term for physical activities as explained in the previous paragraph, while workout, on the other hand, refers more specifically to a set of physical exercises which follow a certain pattern.

When it comes to losing weight, exercises and workouts are a very effective way of achieving your body goals. Though more strenuous, they can be more effective than depending on diet alone. Regular exercises also help prevent or even reverse the effects of some diseases. It reduced the risk of suffering a heart attack and also of developing colon and breast cancer.

Most importantly, exercises are crucial to achieving and maintaining weight loss. They increase rates of metabolism and lean body mass. Also, they can be very beneficial to your mental health as they give a sense of wellbeing, and improved confidence, hence lowering anxiety and depression.

There are many types of exercises which you can do. But for the sake of weight loss, I will classify the best ones under two headings – Aerobic exercises and weight training.

Aerobic Exercises

Aerobic is always associated with oxygen and refers to anything in which oxygen is involved. Aerobic exercises, therefore, refer to any type of physical activity of moderate intensity, which, when being done, can be sustained for more than just a few minutes. It is done mainly to improve cardio-respiratory fitness and overall health.

Aerobic exercises are always accompanied by harder thumping of the heart and faster breathing than when at rest. However, you can sustain the activities for longer periods of time despite this. Your exercise programs should always contain a form of aerobic or cardiovascular exercise. Examples of some of them are walking, jogging, dancing, cycling and swimming. More include working on machines such as treadmill, elliptical, or stair stepper.

Aerobic exercises also make you sweat, which is the byproduct of a faster heartbeat and harder breathing. These exercises improve your cardiovascular health and help deliver oxygen all over the body more efficiently. They are also very effective for weight loss as many body fats are used. In fact, aerobic exercises are best for weight loss, especially as they are a lot easier to follow and don't always require any special equipment to be applied.

Some major benefits of aerobic exercises include;

- **Weight loss:** Due to the nature of the exercises, aerobic exercises' ultimate result is helping you lose some weight.
- **Reduced body fats:** Fat deposits are also affected, and aerobic exercises clear away the extra unwanted ones. This also prevents the accumulation of fat.
- **Increased energy.**
- **Boosted blood circulation:** With your body mass being reduced and as your heart thumps during aerobic exercises, your blood is pumped and circulated at a better rate.
- **Reduction of tension and anxiety:** As blood circulation is boosted, it causes the release of happy hormones, which keeps you in a good mood. This is also vital in curing depression.
- **Improved sleep:** Aerobic exercises calm down the brain and many nerves, thereby improving your sleep.
- **Increased endurance:** Although they can be quite tiring, the moment you begin to get used to them, you can go for longer periods, proving that your endurance has been increased. This increased endurance can be noted and useful in your everyday activities as well.

- **Building a stronger body:** Your entire body is strengthened by performing aerobic exercises in the long run.

If you always lack time, then aerobic exercises are perfect for you since you do not require any special equipment, ingredients, etc. This low requirement makes aerobic exercise one of the most compatible forms of exercise and method of weight loss. Shortly after beginning aerobics, you will feel a notable difference in your energy level, and your skin begins to glow as well. For best results, remember to do aerobics with your diet.

There are many exercises you can do under aerobics. The choice of which and how to combine depends on you. The following are aerobics to help you lose weight quickly.

Skipping: Stand erect and open your feet a little. Grip the jump rope firmly, swing it over your head and jump as soon as it nears the front of your feet. Keep repeating.

Skipping is very easy to do and very effective as well, as it can burn about 450 calories just by doing it for only 45 minutes. It also works on muscles in the shoulders, calves, glutes, and quads.

Jumping Jacks: This is a total body exercise that works mainly on the quads. It also affects the shoulders, abdominals, groin, back, hamstring, outer thighs, and calves. You can shed about 200 calories by doing this exercise for only 20 minutes.

To work with this exercise, stand erect with your feet together while your hands are at either side of your thighs. Jump up and simultaneously spread your feet sideways and your hands above your head. You can do them in sessions of about 10 minutes, with 5 minutes rest in between sessions.

Stair Training: This is a very effective aerobic that tones your lower body and boosts your overall stamina. To do it, you walk up and down the stairs at a steady pace. Try to speed up your motion during the process while maintaining your balance.

Butt Kicks: Stand with both feet apart from each other shoulder width. Bend your arms towards the sides. Bend your right knee like when jogging and touch your butt using your right ankle. Please do the same with the other leg and alternate between them. You can complete 2 or 3 sets of about 30 seconds to 1 minute long each. Remember to keep the pace slow and increase it gradually.

Burpees: It is an intense exercise that affects your entire body. It increases blood circulation, heart rate, and strength, and flexibility. To do it, stand with both your feet apart shoulder width, then get into a squat position. Bend forward, placing your palms in front of your feet, then straighten your feet behind to imitate a plank position. Return to the squat position immediately, then jump. Do 8-15 reps in about 3-5 sets.

Squat Jacks: Keep your feet together and your hands beside your thighs while standing. Jump, spread your feet, and settle into a squat position. Jump back to the starting position pushing through your heels. Do 8-15 reps in about 1-2 sets.

High Knees: Stand, putting your feet apart shoulder width. Lift your knees to your waist level, then slowly drop it. Repeat with the other leg, and keep alternating. Do sets of 30 seconds for as long as you can.

Flutter Kicks: This is very effective in working abs and reducing waistline. To do it, like down facing up, with your hands behind your lower back to give you support. Life up your legs until perpendicular to the ground. Kick up your feet up and down repeatedly. Do about 18-20 reps and complete 2-3 sets.

Invisible Rope Jump: It is similar to skipping but doesn't require a rope. Do this like you are skipping, mimicking every movement. But do not jump more than 2 inches above the ground.

Jump Forward Jogs: keep your feet apart hip wide. Swing arms behind and the forward. Take a giant leap and land softly on your toes. Jog back to starting position and repeat for as long as you want to.

WEIGHT TRAINING

Weight training (resistance training) is simply using weight to tone the body or lose weight. It has been in existence for centuries as a way of building muscular strength. It is also very effective in losing weight by increasing after-burn. It increases muscle size and increases the number of calories that are burnt while we rest.

When exercising, more energy is needed by our muscles than when we are resting. This is because the muscles have the ability to break down fat and carbohydrates that are stored within the muscles. This phenomenon of oxygen intake to remain elevated for muscles to be restored to their state of rest by the burning of stored fats and carbs is known as the after-burn effect.

The amount of fat burnt depends on the after-burn duration, which is dependent on the type, length and intensity of exercise, fitness level, and diet. If the exercise lasts longer, affects more large muscles, and is done to near fatigue, the resulted after-burn lasts longer, and hence more fats and carbohydrates are burnt, causing greater weight loss.

Weight training can be a very effective method of long-term weight control. This is because muscle size is the main factor that decides the Resting Metabolic Rate (RMR) or the amount of calories burnt by your body while resting. For a fact, RMR is responsible for about 60-75% of the total expended energy in non-exercising people. Also, fat is the preferred source of energy of the body at rest.

When doing weight training, make sure the largest muscle groups are engaged, and you should preferably use whole-body exercises, which affects two or more while standing. Due to this, the amount of muscle, hence RMR, is increased as the body is made to work harder. If you are serious about losing a big deal of fats with weight training, your program should have intensity, volume, with a good number of reps and sets, and finally, progression. All these should be high enough to ensure you feel challenged during your workouts and should be increased as you get stronger.

The most effective way of using weights is by employing the repetition method, which is done by performing 6-10 reps with resistance high enough to cause fatigue and makes a succeeding repetition more difficult than the last. This should be done in 3-4 sets and about 2-3 times a week for each muscle group.

One of the major advantages of training with weight is that as you shed fat, you also build muscle. In turn, muscles burn more calories, keeping your weight off for an extended time. The major muscle groups should be worked about thrice a week, and they include; shoulders, chest, abs, forearms, biceps, back, hamstrings, triceps, quads, traps and calves.

When it comes to weight training, there is a very wide variety of options for combining different weight exercises to get the right workout. However, what is more, important is learning ways to get the best results. Below are some important tips you should know and follow if you want to use weight or resistance training to lose weight.

Invest in Guidance: Working with weights can be a little delicate and may cause you harm if you do not fully understand it. Therefore, getting professional help from experts will greatly reduce the chances of you suffering an accident or spoiling your shape. With that, investing in guidance is definitely a very good investment.

You should consider getting a one-on-one tutor, or if you're not comfortable with that, you should definitely join a class.

If you do not want to spend, at the very least, you can get yourself someone to show you all the vital moves, how to use weight machines, and how to ensure safety.

Life Heavy: Have it in mind that weight training won't be easy. If you start feeling it's too easy, you need to add more weight; else, you'll only be doing what the pros call "lifting to failure".

Make Wise Use of Your Time: Not everyone has enough time to spend on workout. That's okay; you don't have to spend every day working out. If you have only a little time to gym, then focus on workouts that affect bigger and more important muscle groups.

Eat Enough Protein: In building up muscles, protein is the most essential class of food. Therefore, when on weight training, make sure taking diets rich in protein is a big part of your plan. The best part is, lean proteins will keep you full for long and ensuring you don't consume unhealthy food.

Be on Calorie Deficit: The quickest way to lose weight is to eat less than your burn. Therefore, it is advisable to keep your calorie intake at a controlled level or scale up your workouts to burn just enough calories.

Creating Personal Routine

Coming to this point, you must have already learned about multiple ways of losing weight and living a healthier life. However, this could have provoked a little confusion. You may now be wondering what method you should follow or which is most effective for you.

While it's true that not everybody can follow every method, it is also ideal that you combine different techniques in the best ways to lose weight most effectively. You should also create a routine with the methods you've learned so far and stick to it for an extended period of time. Below are some of the things you should do before choosing and hopping on a weight loss routine.

TIPS TO CREATING YOUR IDEAL WEIGHT LOSS ROUTINE

First and foremost, identifying your goal is very important; it is your why. Having some targets to aim for will yield far greater long-term results than when you try to kick off a weight loss routine without setting goals. When setting goals, the best method to use is the SMART method. This helps you to set attainable goals and track your progress.

Specific: Be explicit about your reason. Why do you want to lose that weight? Identify your reasons and list them out. Don't set a goal that is too vague or indefinite.

Measurable: Set goals that can be easily tracked. An instance is increasing the number of minutes you exercise or steps you take.

Attainable: Set goals that achievable. If, for instance, you want to work out for an hour daily, but your lifestyle makes that impossible, then you can start with 20 minutes and see how things go from there. Therefore, you should set realistic goals; perhaps, accomplishing your small goals can give you more motivation to aim for bigger ones, and eventually, you succeed in losing that stubborn weight.

Relevant: Make sure each of your goals is related to the main desire of losing weight.

Time-bound: Always fix a deadline for your goals. This helps you measure your progress and plan better in the long run.

After setting your goals, the next thing is to get motivation. There are many ways of finding the right inspiration, and we have seen that you need the right mindset before you can achieve anything. There are different ways of getting motivated; we have already looked at several of them. You can always discover more ways because different things can motivate different people.

Always choose activities you can cope with to add to your routine. The best type of activities; whether food types for your diet, changes to your lifestyle or exercises, always choose the ones that suit you best. This will ensure the weight loss process is as convenient as possible. *Besides, make sure you visit your doctor, be sure of your health condition, and seek advice if you are to avoid certain exercises, diet meals, and so on due to health conditions.*

In other to increase your ability to cope, it would be very beneficial to celebrate your successes. Effective weight loss is not an easy task, so you should celebrate wins; this will also increase your motivation. Always give yourself credit whenever you accomplish a goal; it was due to your effort anyway, you deserved it. There are different ways to reward yourself. You can go for a bath, massage, or fun night with friends. However, it would be best to avoid celebrations that will be inappropriate or unhealthy for you, such as rewarding yourself with food.

Another vital step you should take is always to plan and prepare for challenges and setbacks. You shouldn't expect everything to go as planned. If you do so, you will be unable to endure setbacks and may give up if things go a little sideways. Develop the mindset that losing weight will not be easy. With this, you can stay motivated no matter what life throws at you.

Finally, when creating your routine, do not just settle for less. I have guided you through many methods, so you can combine them however you like. Combining all these exercises would definitely give you the best weight loss routine anywhere. Your program can include a mixed diet of Keto diet and green smoothies. You can base your diet on these two; however it is comfortable for you. And while on a diet, you can make lifestyle modifications and still put out time to perform regular exercises. By doing this, you have gotten the perfect routine containing programs with the most effective and beneficial ways of losing weight. Now, create a routine which you'd stick to and start losing some weight!

CONCLUSION

As I always say, being overweight is not a crime, neither does it lessen your value as a human. Weight gain has definitely been a problem for many in recent times, and having to carry about too much weight can be quite uncomfortable and pose a huge risk to your health. However, know that it is not always your fault. But overcoming all that weight is in your control, you will have to be deliberate about it to take purposeful actions to shed them off.

Although it may take hard work, dedication, and a drastic lifestyle change, with this guide, there is a 100 percent possibility that you will succeed in the long run if you follow through. This ***Must-Have Weight Loss Guide*** must have opened your mind to the fact that we all have what it takes to beat the weight gain and obesity menace in our beloved country U.S. and the world at large.

I have done my part in offering assistance as a professional; now it's time to do yours. Get your priorities straight, get motivated and dedicate your time and effort to the guides I have given you thus far. Now go out there, and get to lose some weight. Good luck!

NOTES

NOTES